Tutankhamun's Tomb

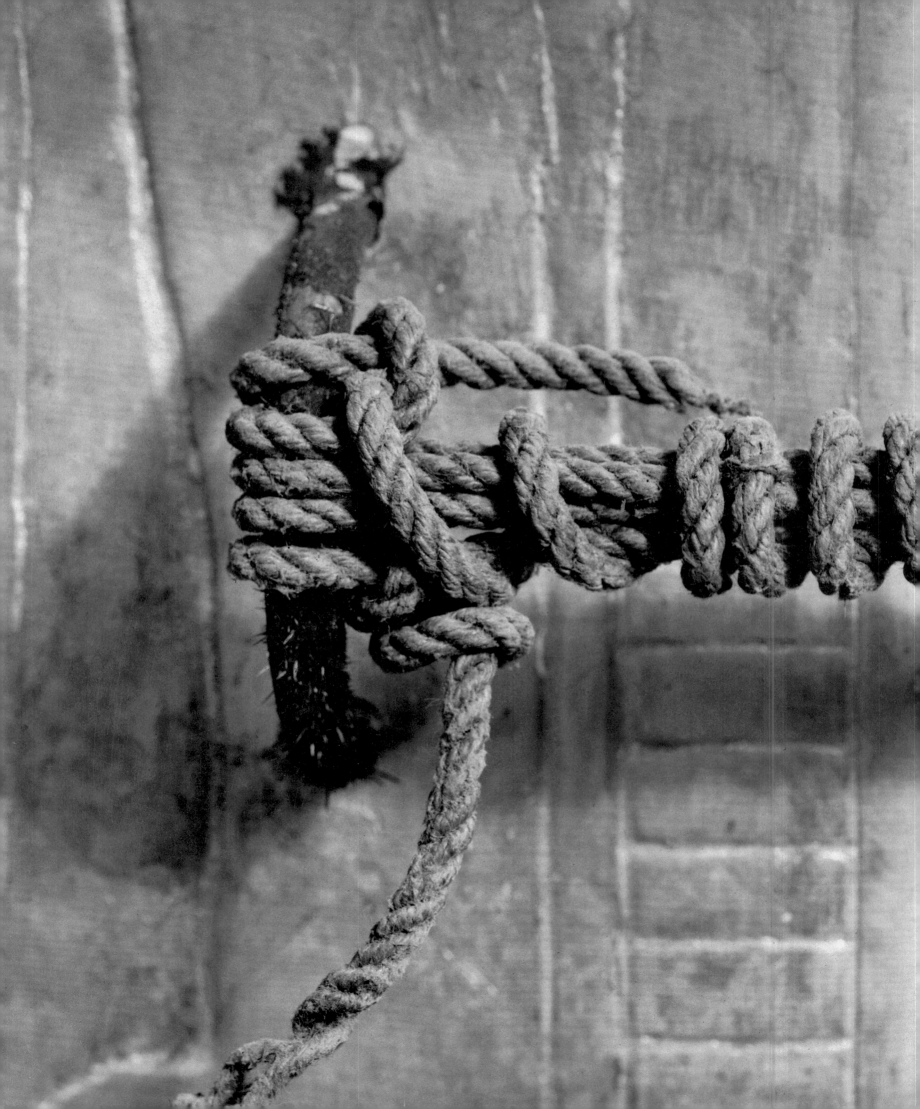

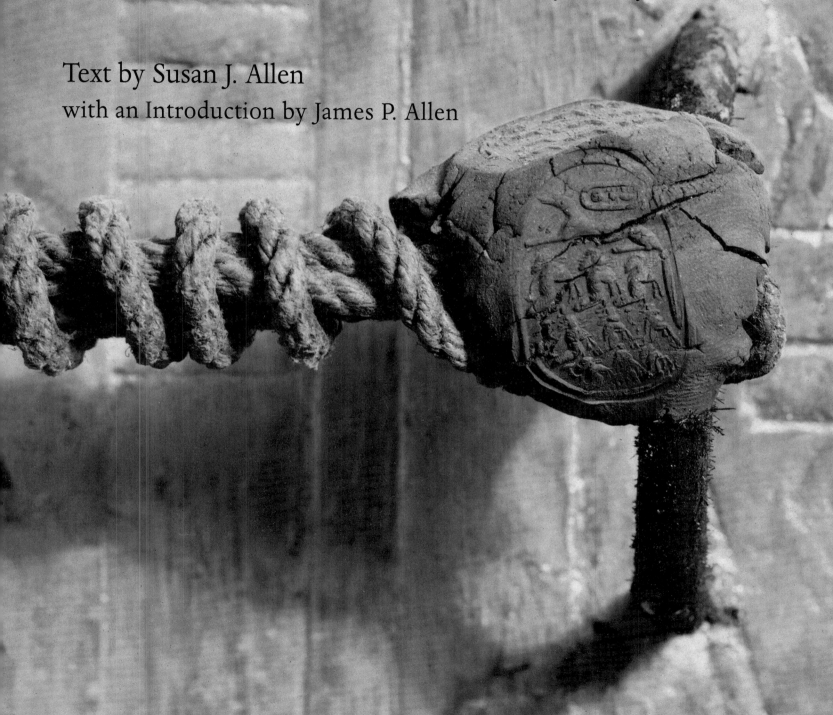

Tutankhamun's Tomb

The Thrill of Discovery   Photographs by Harry Burton

Text by Susan J. Allen
with an Introduction by James P. Allen

THE METROPOLITAN MUSEUM OF ART, NEW YORK

YALE UNIVERSITY PRESS, NEW HAVEN AND LONDON

This volume has been published in conjunction with the exhibitions "Wonderful Things! The Discovery of the Tomb of Tutankhamun,
The Harry Burton Photographs," held at The Oriental Institute Museum, The University of Chicago, May 26–October 8, 2006, and "Tutankhamun's Tomb:
The Thrill of Discovery," held at The Metropolitan Museum of Art, New York, December 19, 2006–April 29, 2007.

Published by The Metropolitan Museum of Art, New York
Copyright © 2006 by The Metropolitan Museum of Art, New York

John P. O'Neill, Editor in Chief
Gwen Roginsky, Associate General Manager of Publications
Ellen Shultz, Editor
Bruce Campbell, Designer
Christopher Zichello, Production Manager
Robert Weisberg, Assistant Managing Editor

Cataloguing-in-Publication Data is available from the Library of Congress.
ISBN 1-58839-189-2 (hc: The Metropolitan Museum of Art)
ISBN 0-300-12026-5 (hc: Yale University Press)

Plates 2, 6, 21, 25, 27–30, 52, Copyright Griffith Institute, Oxford
Plates 38, 39, Copyright of Times Newspapers Ltd
Map of the Theban necropolis and plan of the tomb by Anandaroop Roy
Frontispiece/Title page: Detail of plate 34 (MMA Burton photo TAA 622)
Page 8: MMA Burton photo 211301

Printed and bound by EBS Editoriale Bortolazzi-Stei s.r.l., Verona

Contents

Director's Foreword

The discovery of the tomb of Tutankhamun in 1922 by the British archaeologist Howard Carter and his benefactor Lord Carnarvon continues to fascinate us. The newspapers of the time featured articles almost daily, augmented by lavish photo spreads, monitoring the progress of the excavations. Carter himself published a three-volume account of the discovery, although scholarly publications devoted to the tomb and its contents continue to this day. Four international exhibitions of objects from the tomb, held over the past forty years, have periodically renewed interest in Tutankhamun, drawing record crowds of spectators.

The Metropolitan Museum's team was fortunate not only to have been present at the site in 1922 but also to have had the resources to assist Carter in the meticulous documentation and clearance of the thousands of items in the tomb. At their meeting in January 1923, the Museum's trustees confirmed this arrangement, stating their "desire to express to his Lordship [Carnarvon] their appreciation of the honor he has done the members of the Museum's staff in selecting them for assistance in this very important and delicate work." First and foremost, the Museum volunteered the services of Harry Burton—one of the best archaeological photographers ever—to the enterprise. He produced a photographic record of the objects as they appeared when he found them in the tomb and, again, after they had been transferred to the studio, cleaned, and repaired. A set of these prints and negatives now resides in the archives of the Metropolitan Museum's Department of Egyptian Art and in its Photograph Studio; another set, along with Carter's notes, belongs to the Griffith Institute at The University of Oxford in England.

The selection of the Burton gelatin silver prints that illustrate this volume shows the excitement Carter and his team undoubtedly felt as they penetrated the tomb, disentangling the delicate jumble of objects that had been crammed into its four small rooms—unfortunately, subsequently disturbed by grave robbers— and opening the multitude of chests and boxes filled with the jewelry and personal possessions of the young king. Burton's photographs also capture that moment in time, more than thirty-three hundred years ago, when the last ancient Egyptian necropolis official prepared to take his leave of the tomb, for what he hoped would be eternity, checking one final time to see that its magical contents had been strategically placed to protect the spirit of the dead pharaoh, and that the boxes were closed, before the doors were sealed.

The mission of the Metropolitan Museum is not only to preserve and display art objects but also to document them and provide explanations and interpretations of their original functions and contexts. The photographs of Harry Burton demonstrate the Museum's commitment to recording and preserving the past for the edification and enjoyment of future generations.

Philippe de Montebello
Director, The Metropolitan Museum of Art

Acknowledgments

A great many people have contributed to the production of this volume. The authors are grateful to Emily Teeter, Research Associate at The Oriental Institute Museum, The University of Chicago, whose idea for an exhibition emphasizing the archaeological importance of Harry Burton's photographs of the tomb of Tutankhamun provided the initial impetus for the publication of this book. The authors also wish to thank the Griffith Institute at The University of Oxford for permission to use additional Burton photographs, not in the Metropolitan Museum's collection, in this publication; and Dr. Jaromir Malek, for his long dedication to the Tutankhamun archive at the Griffith, which has been made accessible worldwide on their website, Tutankhamun: Anatomy of an Excavation.

Burton's black-and-white photographs of the tomb of Tutankhamun were first exhibited at the Metropolitan Museum in the spring of 1923. In addition, Burton made the first motion pictures of the removal of objects from the tomb. Many of these images have been reproduced over the years, and are familiar to the interested reader. In 1991, Marsha Hill, Curator in the Metropolitan Museum's Department of Egyptian Art, prepared a biographical study of Harry Burton to accompany the publication of his photographs of the tomb of Seti I. In September 2001, the Museum mounted another exhibition of Burton's work, "The Pharaoh's Photographer: Harry Burton, Tutankhamun, and the Metropolitan's Egyptian Expedition," organized jointly by Catharine Roehrig, Curator, Department of Egyptian Art, and Malcolm Daniel, Curator in Charge, Department of Photographs. The present authors are indebted to these earlier publications and exhibitions, which aided their research for this book.

This volume was produced by the Museum's Editorial Department, under the direction of John P. O'Neill, Editor in Chief and General Manager of Publications. It was edited by Ellen Shultz, designed by Bruce Campbell, and produced by Gwen Roginsky, Associate General Manager of Publications, and Christopher Zichello. The tomb plan and the map of Thebes were drawn by Anandaroop Roy. Robert Goldman, Assistant Photographer, and Barbara Bridgers, General Manager for Imaging and Photography, The Photograph Studio, are responsible for the masterful digital imaging of Burton's original prints.

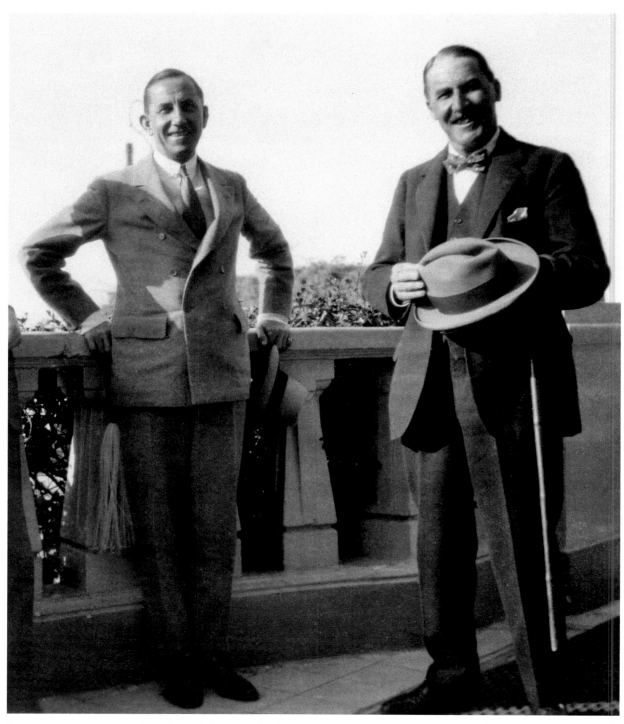

Posing on the terrace of the Winter Palace Hotel in Luxor are Howard Carter (right), who discovered the tomb of Tutankhamun, and Harry Burton (left), the official photographer of the tomb, whose services were lent to Carter by The Metropolitan Museum of Art Egyptian Expedition.

INTRODUCTION

by James P. Allen

The photographs in this book capture one of the most memorable episodes in the history of archaeology: the discovery of the tomb of the ancient Egyptian pharaoh Tutankhamun (Dynasty 18; ruled about 1336–1327 B.C.). They offer an unparalleled view of that discovery, allowing us not only to see the tomb's treasures as they appeared when found but also to experience some of the excitement and awe felt by the excavators themselves.

The tomb of Tutankhamun lies in the Valley of the Kings (see map, p. 13), behind the cliffs west of the modern city of Luxor (ancient Thebes). Between 1898 and 1914, exploration of the valley resulted in the identification of sixty-one tombs, among them the burial places of most of the pharaohs who had ruled Egypt during Dynasties 18 to 20 (from about 1550 to 1070 B.C.). The last tomb to be discovered before Tutankhamun's, that of Haremhab (Dynasty 18; ruled about 1323–1295 B.C.), was found in 1908 by an expedition financed by the American businessman Theodore M. Davis (1837–1915). Davis continued to participate in excavations for six more years; he retired in 1914, noting: "I fear that the Valley of the Tombs is now exhausted."[1]

Davis's pessimism was not shared by other archaeologists. In 1915, exploration in the Valley of the Kings was taken up by a new expedition, financed by George Edward Stanhope Molyneux Herbert, 5th Earl of Carnarvon (1866–1923), and led by the British Egyptologist Howard Carter (1873–1939). Carter spent six seasons in the valley in search of an undiscovered royal tomb, but by the spring of 1922 he still had little to show for his efforts other than fragments of funerary statues and other burial equipment left behind by tomb robbers. A short season in the final two months of that year was to be his last.

On November 1, 1922, Carter began clearing the remains of huts used by ancient workmen near the entrance to the tomb of Ramesses VI (plate 3). Three days later, on the morning of November 4, he discovered the first of what would prove to be sixteen steps cut into the valley floor (plate 4). By sunset on November 5, his workmen had cleared twelve of these steps and exposed the top of a blocked doorway, sealed in plaster and stamped with the insignia of the royal necropolis. At this point, Carter was uncertain of exactly what he had discovered: "Could it be the tomb of a noble, buried there by royal consent? Or was it a royal cache? As far as my investigations had gone there was absolutely nothing to tell me . . . but as it was, it was getting late, the night had fast set in, the full moon had risen high in the eastern heavens. I refilled the excavation for protection . . . and cabled to L[or]d C[arnarvon] (then in England) the following message: 'At last have made wonderful discovery in Valley a magnificent tomb with seals intact recovered same for your arrival congratulations.'"[2] On November 24, a day after Carnarvon's arrival, the rubble had been removed from the stairs and doorway, revealing seals of Tutankhamun stamped into the plastered façade of the stones blocking the entrance. The next day, Carter began excavation of the tomb.

Carter's diary for November 25 contains the note: "Made photographic records, which were not, as they afterwards proved, very successful." Perhaps, for this reason, he decided to seek assistance from The Metropolitan Museum of Art's expedition, which was excavating at the time in the Theban necropolis. On December 7, during a trip to Cairo to order excavation supplies, he cabled Albert M. Lythgoe (1868–1934), head of the Museum's Department of Egyptian Art: "[D]iscovery colossal and need every assistance could you consider loan of Burton in recording in time being costs to us immediate reply would oblige every regards Carter." Lythgoe replied the same day: "Only too delighted to assist in every possible way. Please call upon Burton and any other members of our staff. Am cabling Burton to that effect. Lythgoe."[3] In the end, the Museum lent Carter the services not only of its photographer Harry Burton (see plate on p. 8) but also those of three other members of its Theban expedition: artist Lindsley F. Hall (1883–1969), architect Walter Hauser (1893–1959), and Egyptologist Arthur C. Mace (1874–1928). Carter credited Mace as coauthor of his initial report on the discovery of the tomb,[4] but Burton's photographs have provided the most enduring legacy of the excavation.

Harry Burton (1879–1940) acquired a reputation as a photographer of art during the years he spent in Florence, where he was the protégé of, and secretary to, an art historian.[5] While in Florence he met Theodore M. Davis, and in 1910 he was engaged to direct Davis's excavations in Thebes. Upon Davis's retirement in 1914, Burton was hired by the Metropolitan Museum's Department of Egyptian Art to undertake a photographic record of Theban monuments. As part of this task, he introduced the use of color photography to record archaeological sites. Burton remained with the Museum until his death, although between 1922 and 1933 he spent much of his time in Egypt, documenting Carter's excavation and clearance of the tomb of Tutankhamun.

That tomb is one of the smallest in the Valley of the Kings. Behind the blocked doorway at the bottom of the stairs, a corridor twenty-five feet long and five-and-a-half feet wide extends westward; when found, it was filled with debris. At the end of the corridor there stood a small head of the king (plate 5), outside the blocked entrance to the tomb's first room, known as the Antechamber. The Antechamber itself, nearly twenty-six feet wide and eleven-and-a-half feet deep, was filled with tomb furniture (see plates 7, 9, 10, 18). A small opening in its west wall (plate 71), originally blocked and plastered shut, led to a room fourteen feet wide by eight-and-a-half feet long, which Carter called the Annex; this, too, was filled with furniture (plate 73). In the north wall of the Antechamber is another entrance, also discovered sealed (plates 18, 21), which opens into the Burial Chamber, twenty-one feet long and thirteen-and-a-half feet wide. When Carter removed the rubble blocking the entrance, he came upon what seemed like a solid wall of gold (see plate 22). This proved to be the outermost of four shrines (plate 26), which was so large that it left less than three feet between its side walls and those of the Burial Chamber. Within the shrines lay the sarcophagus containing the three nested coffins and the mummy of Tutankhamun (see plates 40–45). From the north wall of the Burial Chamber, an open doorway leads to the last room in the tomb (plate 49), fifteen-and-a-half feet wide and twelve-and-a-half feet deep, which Carter called the Treasury; its primary function was to house the shrine containing the king's internal organs (plates 57–59).

Tutankhamun's tomb eventually yielded 5,398 separate finds, ranging from tiny beads to massive shrines, and from simple pottery to the king's innermost coffin of solid gold. These are among the most famous and iconic objects of Egyptian art ever to have been discovered. Even more significant than their artistic value, however, is what they have revealed about Tutankhamun himself. Before the tomb's discovery, Tutankhamun was known only as an ephemeral king, who had ruled for a few years at the end of the Eighteenth Dynasty. The brief length of his reign even suggested that he had come to the throne at an advanced age. Inscriptions from his tomb, however, have indicated that he ruled for nine or ten years, and his mummy has revealed that he died at about the age of nineteen. Some of the furniture and clothing buried with him were suitable for a child of ten or eleven—Tutankhamun's age when he was crowned king.

Heirlooms and other objects from the tomb have also shed light on the turbulent reign of Tutankhamun's immediate predecessors, including the "heretic" pharaoh Akhenaten, who attempted to reform Egyptian religion by introducing the worship of a single god. Tutankhamun eventually married Akhenaten's third daughter, Ankhesenamun, who is depicted with the young king on a number of items from the tomb (see plates 32, 77). Elements of Tutankhamun's burial equipment, such as his sarcophagus, middle coffin, and canopic shrine and coffins (plates 40, 42, 43, 59, 60), were originally made for a predecessor named Neferneferuaten; she was probably a daughter of Akhenaten, who ruled as a pharaoh with her father.

When the tomb was discovered, Egyptologists hoped that it would contain papyri or other historical records of this puzzling episode in Egyptian history, but that expectation was not to be realized. As with most archaeological discoveries, Tutankhamun's tomb has perhaps raised as many new questions as it has answered old ones. Among its treasures are those created for, or dedicated by, Tutankhamun's predecessors and contemporaries, but none of these tells who his father or mother were. Other objects belonged to Tutankhamun personally, but their use and significance remain a mystery: for example, the armless, wood half-length bust of the king (plate 11).

Harry Burton recorded all of the tomb's finds in a series of some fourteen hundred glass-plate negatives, which are preserved today in the archives of The Metropolitan Museum of Art and in Great Britain at the Griffith Institute in Oxford. His photographs record the objects not only after they were cleaned and conserved but also as they appeared when first encountered. Like all of Burton's work, these images are remarkable for their clarity and evenness of lighting. Burton preferred sunlight to artificial illumination; when photographing inside a tomb, he used a series of mirrors and reflectors to direct the light inward so that it was diffused over the subject. The result is often so clear and sharp that the details stand out even when viewed under the microscope.

Burton's photographs also present the tomb as Carter first saw it. They preserve elements that were necessarily lost or altered in the course of excavation, such as the blocked entrances to the tomb chambers, the arrangement of items in the various rooms, and the elaborate, sealed knot on the doors of each shrine (see plate 34). Burton also recorded the process of excavation, allowing us to witness Carter opening the second shrine (plate 35), viewing the king's second coffin (plate 43), and examining the mummy of Tutankhamun (plate 46). The experience is even more immediate in the motion pictures that Burton made of the excavation. These films, housed today in the Metropolitan Museum's archives, represent the first archaeological use of the medium, which Burton learned in Hollywood during the summer of 1924 and employed in subsequent seasons to record both the Museum's and Carter's excavations.

The discovery of the tomb of Tutankhamun was a singular event in Egyptian archaeology and perhaps one that will never be equaled. Like the world of Tutankhamun itself, this moment in time has passed irrevocably into history, but in the photographs of Harry Burton it is preserved for posterity.

1. T. M. Davis, *The Tombs of Harmhabi and Touatânkhamanou* (London: Constable, 1912), p. 3.

2. H. Carter, *Notes, Diary, and Articles, Referring to the Theban Royal Necropolis and the Tomb of Tutankhamen* (Oxford: Griffith Institute Archive i.2.1, n.d.), cited here courtesy of the Griffith Institute. The diary is available on the internet at http://www.ashmolean.museum/gri/4seainot.html.

3. The two cables, in the archives of the Metropolitan Museum's Department of Egyptian Art, are reproduced in *Wonderful Things: The Discovery of Tutankhamun's Tomb*, ed. P. Cone (New York: The Metropolitan Museum of Art, 1976), pp. xiv–xv.

4. H. E. Carter and A. C. Mace, *The Tomb of Tut·ankh·amen, Discovered by the Late Earl of Carnarvon and Howard Carter*, 3 vols. (New York: Doran, 1923–33).

5. For more extensive details on Burton's life and career, see M. Hill, "The Life and Work of Harry Burton," in E. Hornung, *The Tomb of Pharaoh Seti I/Das Grab Sethos' I*. (Zürich and Munich: Artemis, 1991), pp. 27–30.

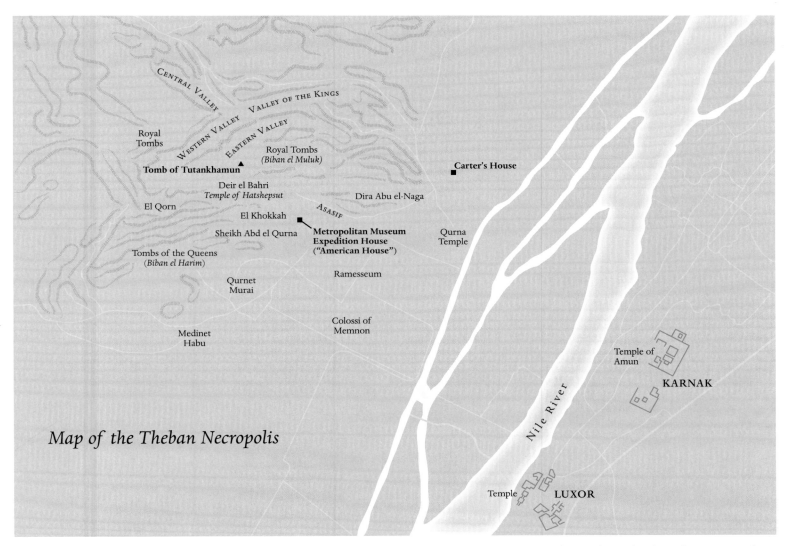

Map of the Theban Necropolis

CENTRAL VALLEY

WESTERN VALLEY VALLEY OF THE KINGS

EASTERN VALLEY

Royal Tombs

Royal Tombs (*Biban el Muluk*)

Carter's House

Tomb of Tutankhamun

Deir el Bahri *Temple of Hatshepsut*

Dira Abu el-Naga

El Qorn

ASASIF

El Khokkah

Sheikh Abd el Qurna

Metropolitan Museum Expedition House ("American House")

Qurna Temple

Tombs of the Queens (*Biban el Harim*)

Ramesseum

Qurnet Murai

Colossi of Memnon

Medinet Habu

Nile River

Temple of Amun

KARNAK

Temple **LUXOR**

The tomb of Tutankhamun was discovered in the main part of the Valley of the Kings. Howard Carter's house, located a short distance outside the Valley, is still standing today. The Metropolitan Museum Expedition House, where Harry Burton and the other staff members lived when they were assisting Carter in the documentation and emptying of the tomb, is situated in Deir el Bahri, directly over the mountain from the Valley; it is now being used by a joint Egyptian-Polish mission that is restoring the mortuary temple of Queen Hatshepsut.

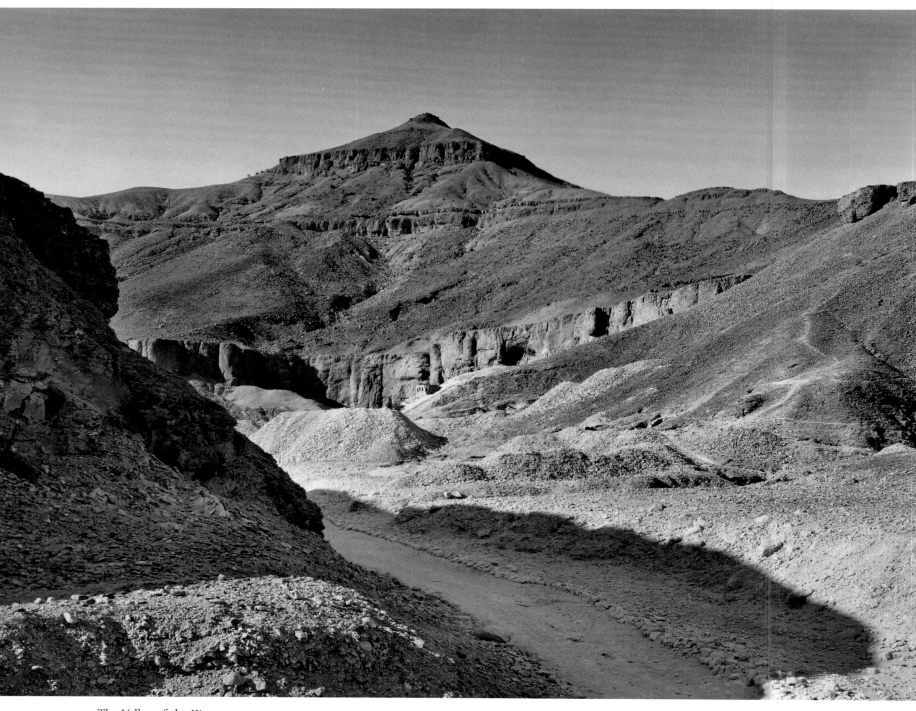

1. The Valley of the Kings

Beginning in 1915, Carter set out to systematically search for the tomb of Tutankhamun. The Valley of the Kings is vast, with many side valleys, and he had only a few meager clues—such as the so-called embalmer's cache of Tutankhamun, found near the tomb of Seti I—to help him narrow the area of his search.

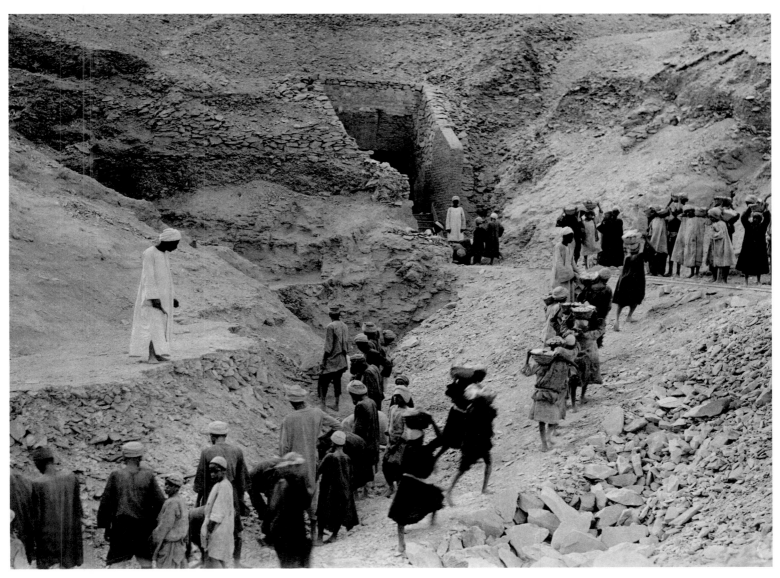

2. Workmen clearing away debris

Year after year, Carter and his workmen shifted the limestone rubble down to bedrock.

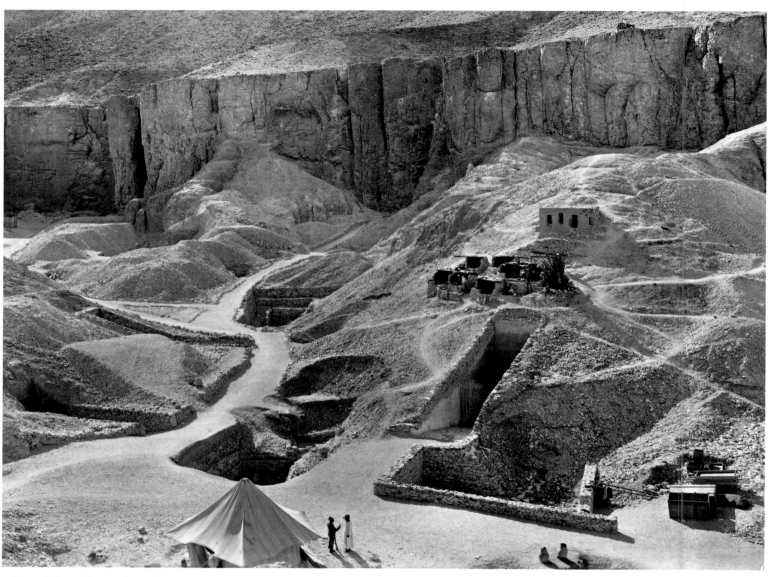

3. Site of Tutankhamun's tomb

Ultimately, only the area below the tomb of Ramesses VI remained. Time and money were running out and the few objects found were uninspiring. Finally, on November 4, 1922, Carter's workmen came upon a step in the bedrock; clearance of the stairs led to a sealed doorway. The thrill of discovery was tempered by the need for patience. The stair was refilled, and Lord Carnarvon, who sponsored Carter's work in the Valley, was summoned from England, but he did not arrive until November 23. Everyone was left to wonder if this tomb, like so many others, had been thoroughly pillaged in antiquity.

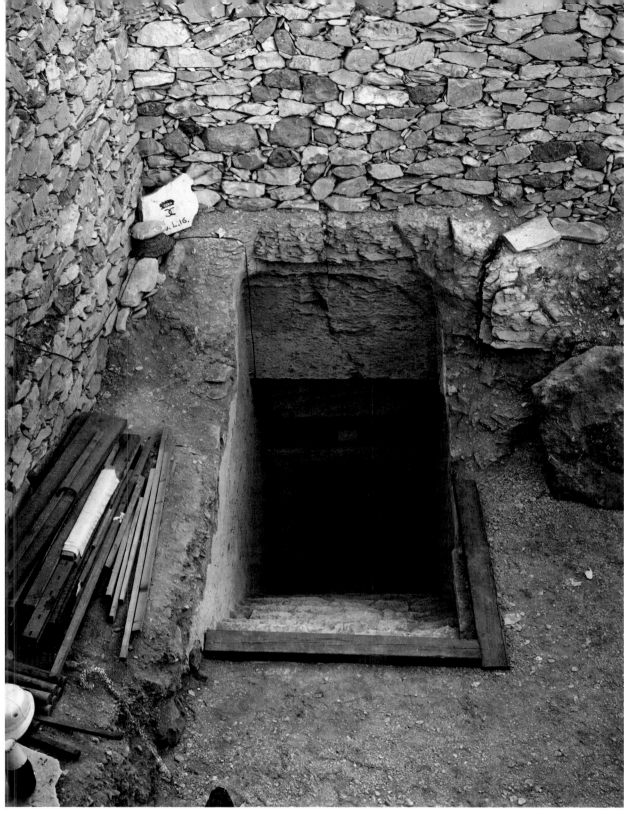

4. Entrance to the tomb

On November 24, the stairway was reexcavated. The outer doorway showed evidence of having been sealed more than once, but it bore the official seals of the necropolis and of Tutankhamun. Carter, an experienced excavator, could tell that the rubble filling the entrance corridor had been tunneled through. This, and the resealing of the door, indicated that the tomb probably had been penetrated or reopened at least once by tomb robbers and resealed by the necropolis officials.

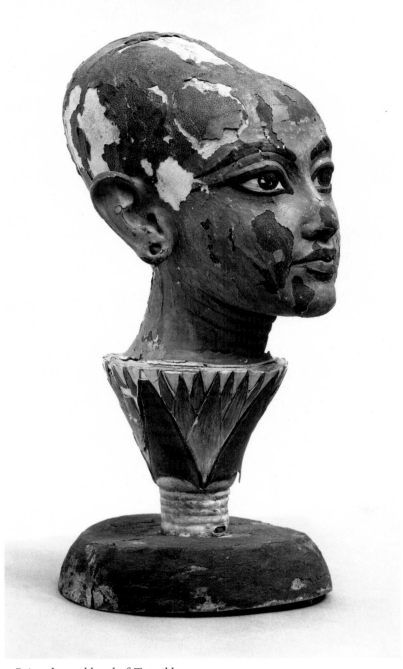

5. Painted wood head of Tutankhamun

After three more days the corridor was cleared, only to reveal another blocked and resealed doorway at the end. In front of this doorway were several pottery vessels and cups and a small painted-wood head of the king as a child, emerging from a lily. Had these objects been left there by the tomb robbers, who deemed them of little value?

6. (Opposite): Passageway to the tomb

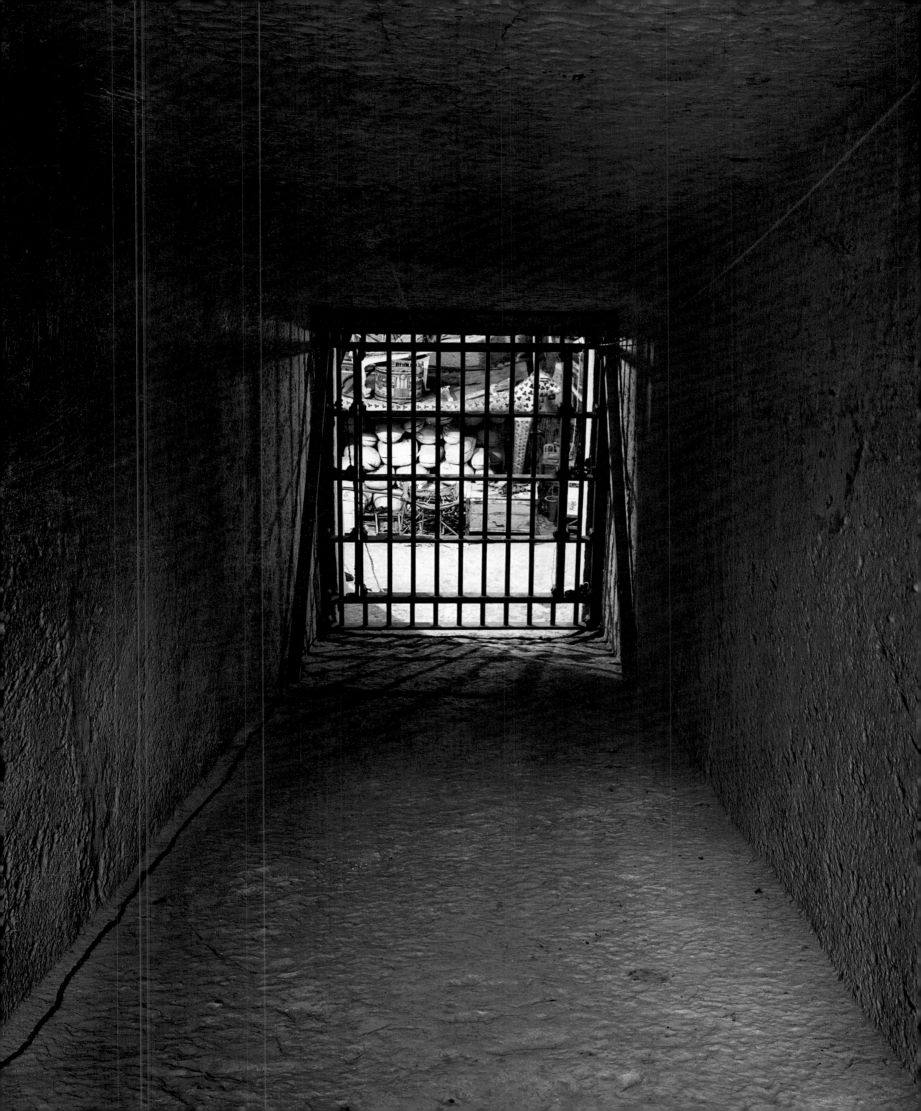

At this point the suspense must have built up to an almost intolerable level. From the discovery of the first step in the bedrock to the breaching of this second doorway, more than three weeks had elapsed. Carefully, Carter made a small hole in the blocking, inserted a candle, and waited for the stale air in the tomb to clear and for his eyes and those of Lord Carnarvon and his daughter Lady Evelyn to adjust.

What they saw must have been both astonishing and thrilling at the same time. The small space beyond the door was crammed with all manner of furniture, boxes, and dismantled chariots, seemingly piled in disarray. The gilded animal heads on the three mammoth ritual couches gleamed eerily in the flickering light. While the tomb clearly had been disturbed, it certainly had not been deliberately vandalized or stripped of its contents. Whether the king himself remained buried there was a question that was still to be resolved. This was only the Antechamber.

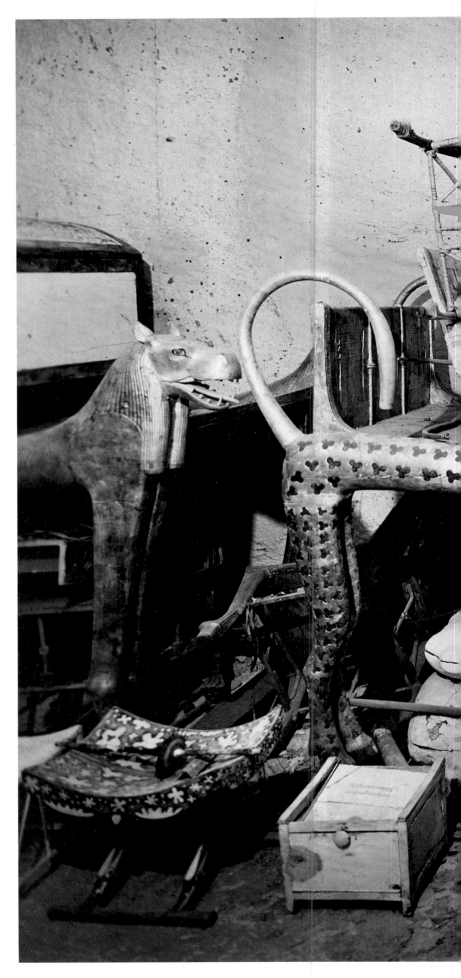

7. The Antechamber

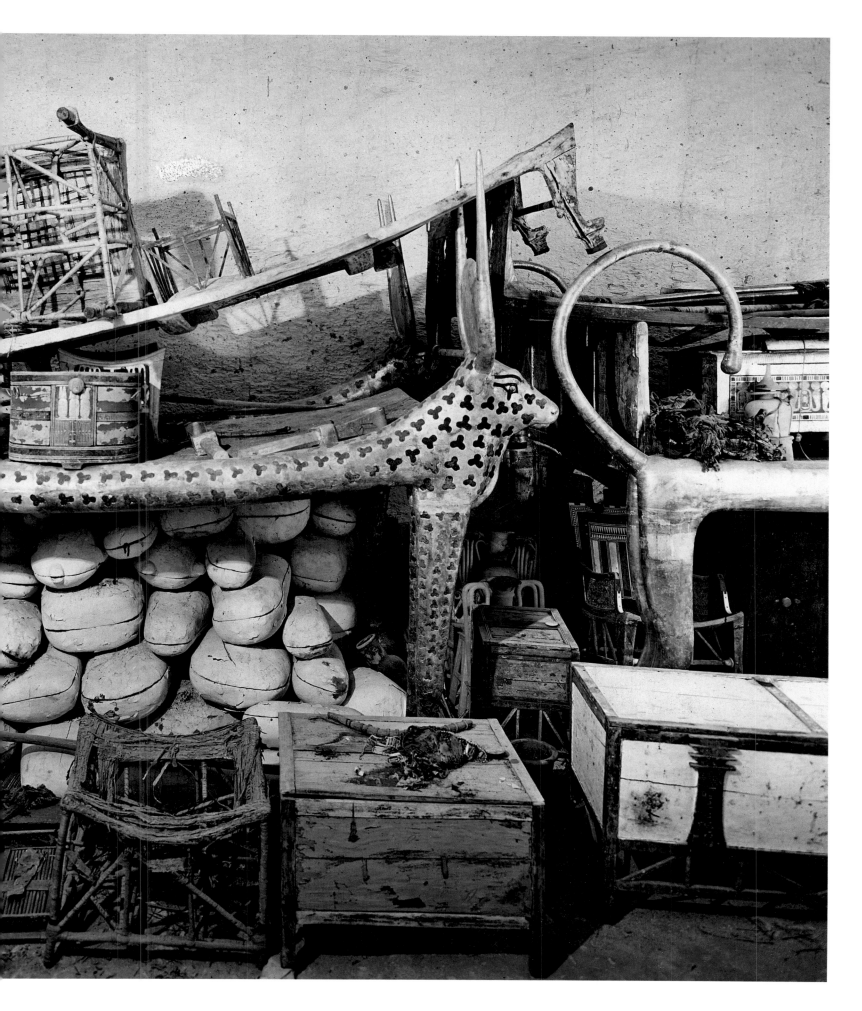

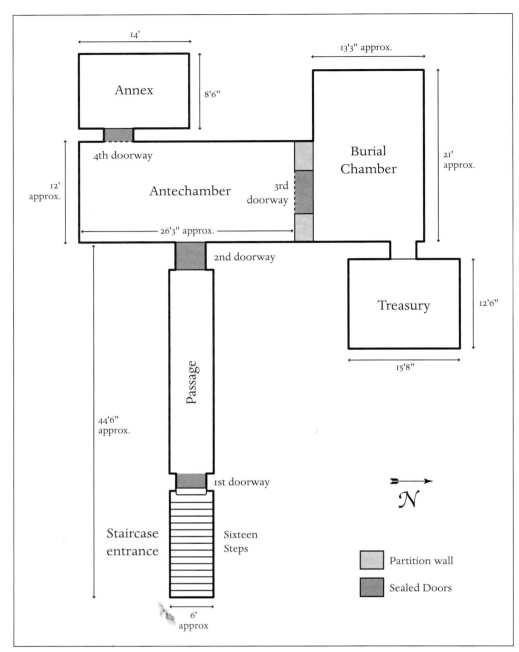

14'

8'6"

Annex

13'3" approx.

4th doorway

12'
approx.

Antechamber

Burial
Chamber

3rd
doorway

21'
approx.

26'3" approx.

2nd doorway

Passage

Treasury

12'6"

15'8"

44'6"
approx.

1st doorway

𝒩

Staircase
entrance

Sixteen
Steps

Partition wall

Sealed Doors

6'
approx

8. Plan of the tomb

Many of the objects in the tomb were very fragile and had lain one on top of the other for more than three thousand years. Each item had to be carefully removed, labeled, and photographed. When an object was shifted it invariably revealed others, such as these elaborate alabaster vessels placed on the floor between the couches.

9. (Opposite): Ointment jars found in the Antechamber

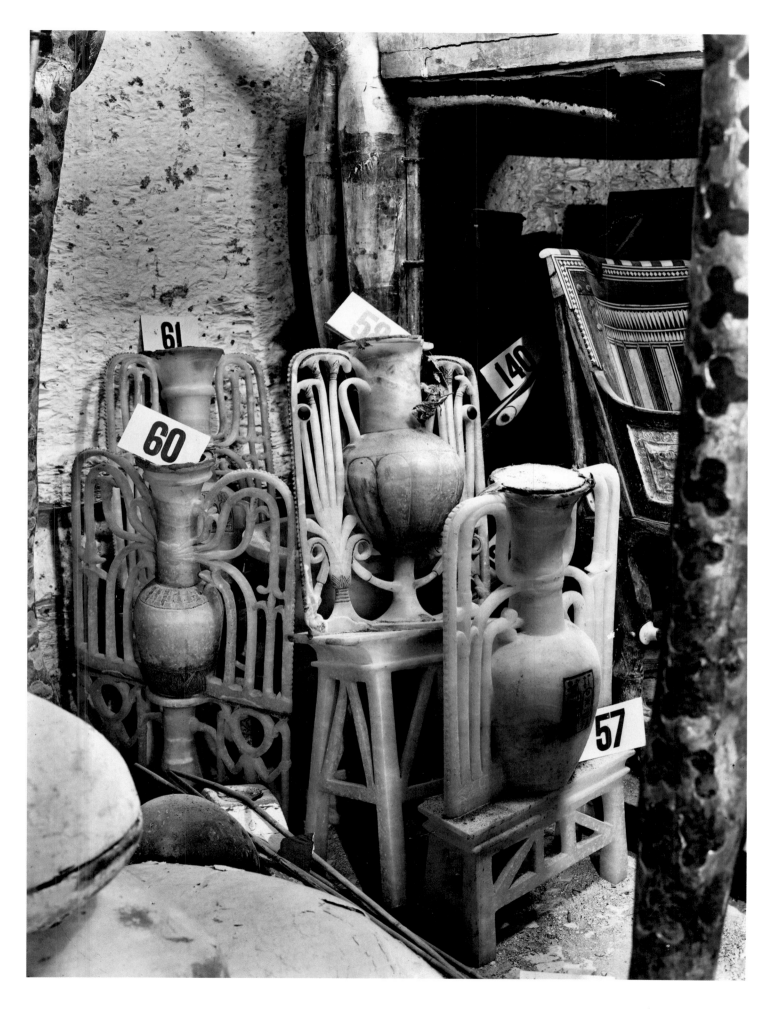

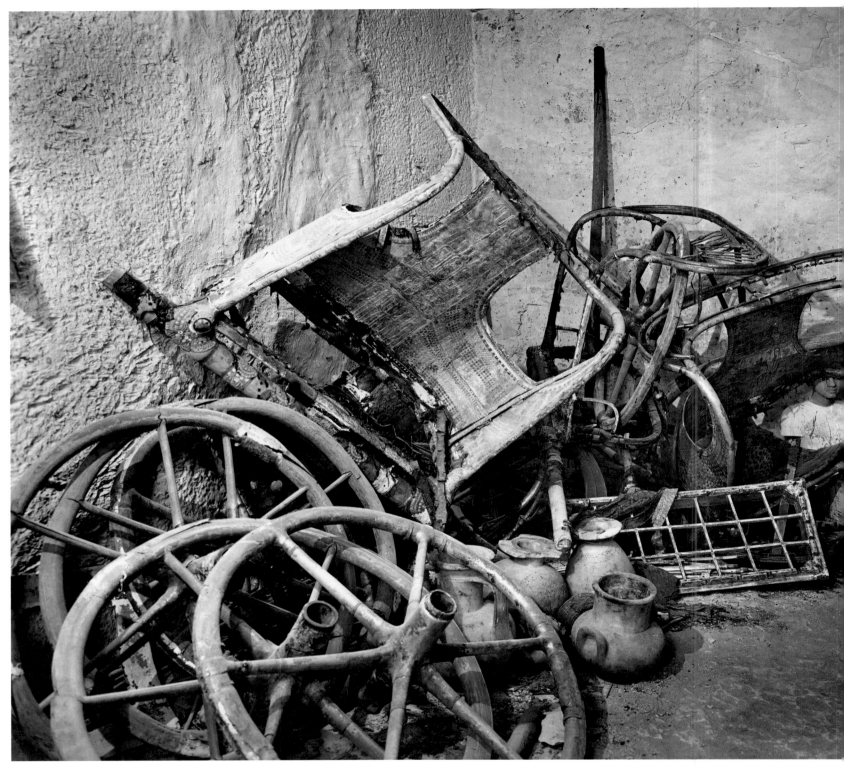

10. Dismantled chariots discovered in the Antechamber

Removal of the disassembled chariots disclosed a simple and elegant wood half-length bust of the young king, which Carter speculated might have served as a sort of mannequin.

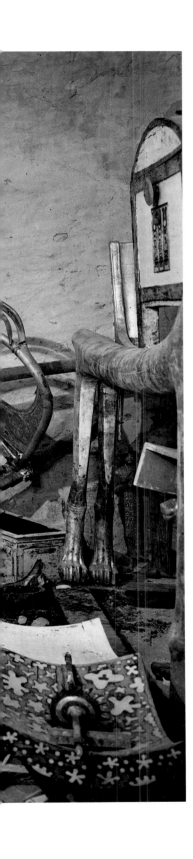

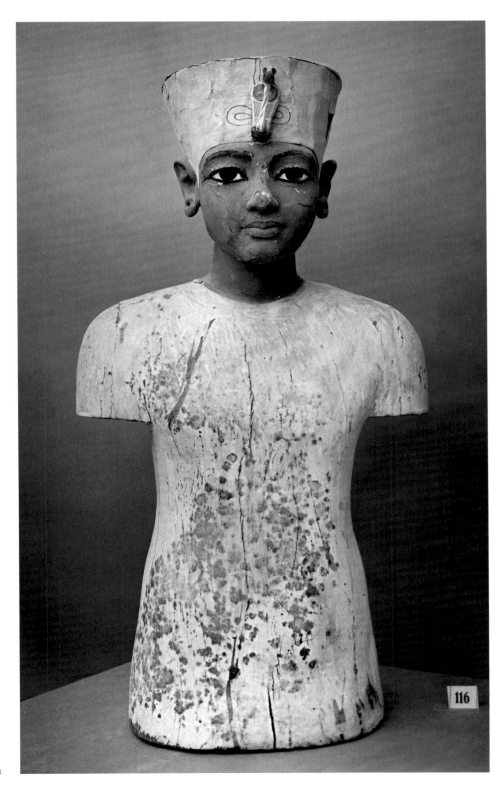

11. Wood half-length bust of Tutankhamun

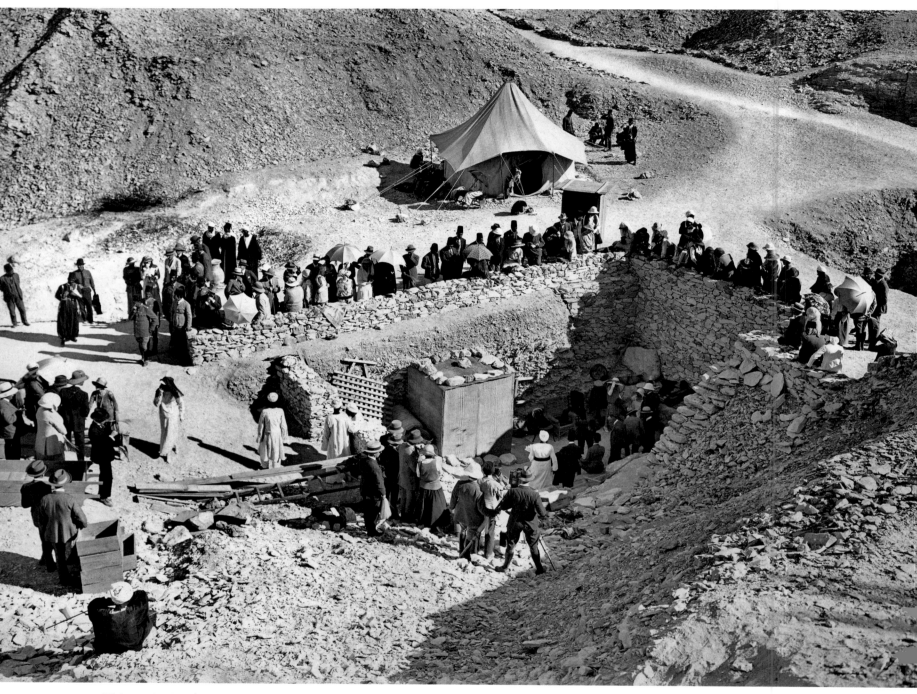

12. Visitors viewing the excavation site

The site of the discovery was soon flooded by the press, tourists, and important personages and officials, all of whom required Carter's personal attention. Elisabeth, Queen of the Belgians, an ardent Egyptophile, was one such special royal visitor.

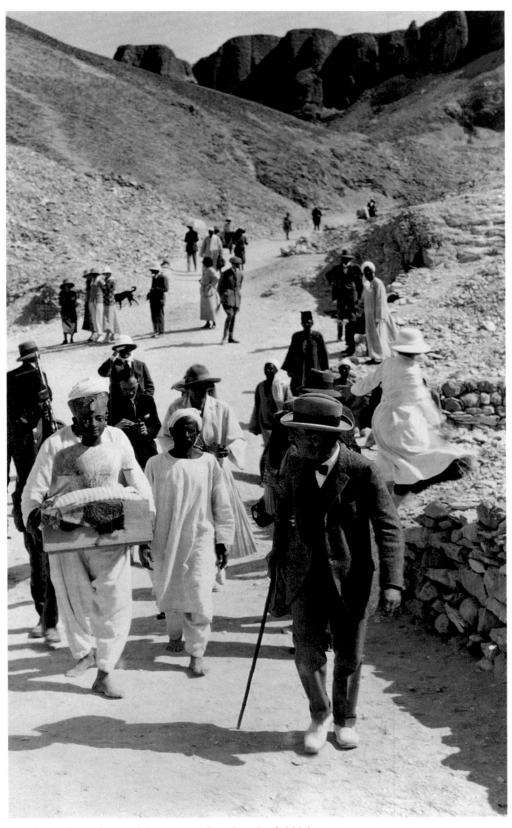

13. Objects from the tomb being transferred to the field laboratory

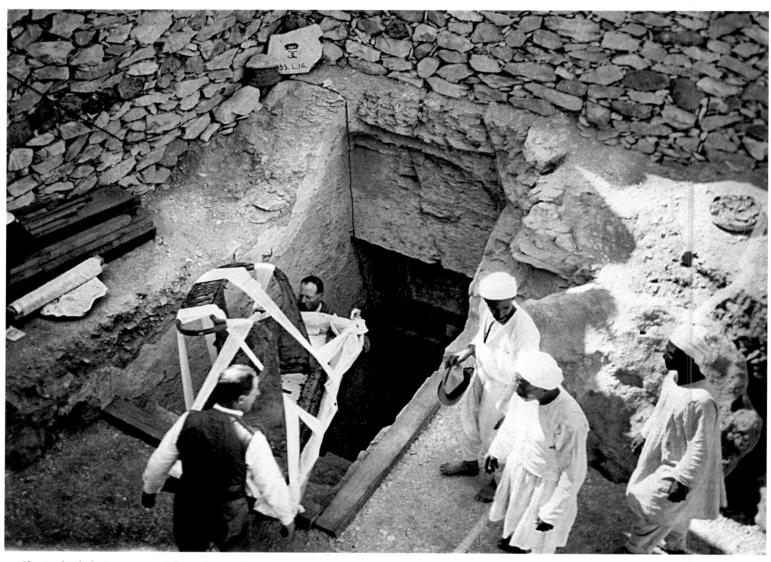

14. Chariot body being removed from the tomb

The contents of the tomb needed to be documented and their location plotted on a floor plan; then they had to be photographed in situ before being handled. Howard Carter was directly involved in every aspect of the work. With the assistance of his good friend Arthur Callender and the staff on loan from the Metropolitan Museum, he wrapped and then moved every item himself. On December 27, the first object was carried out of the Antechamber and, in six weeks, the room had been cleared of all but the two guardian figures flanking the door to the Burial Chamber.

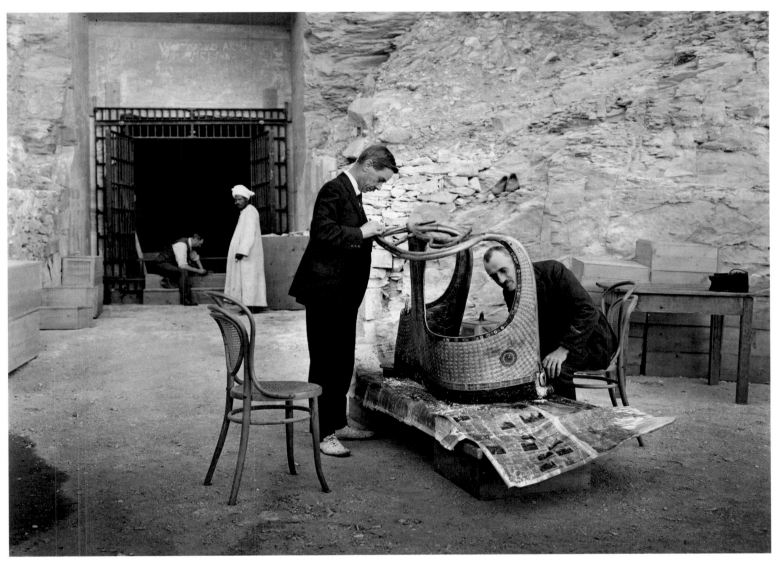

15. Arthur Mace, archaeologist, and Alfred Lucas, chemist, examining a chariot

After the objects were removed from the tomb of Tutankhamun, all of them had to be cleaned, checked for damage, and stabilized prior to being photographed in the studio and prepared for their eventual transfer to the Egyptian Museum in Cairo. A field laboratory was set up in the nearby tomb of Seti II, as the delicate conservation work on the objects could not be performed in the hot, dusty, and cramped space of Tutankhamun's tomb.

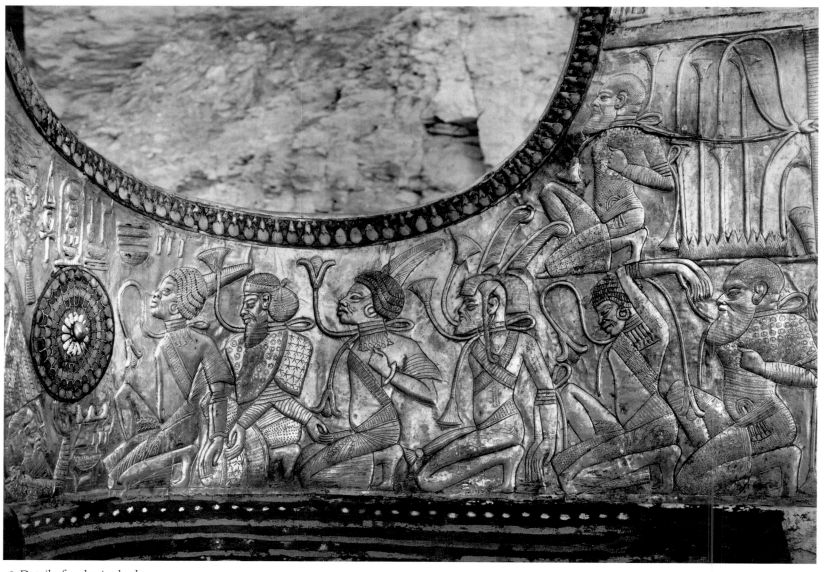

16. Detail of a chariot body

Arthur Mace, a member of the Metropolitan Museum's Egyptian Expedition, and the pioneering archaeological chemist Alfred Lucas cleaned and conserved such fragile objects as the king's chariots, in the process revealing the incredible beauty and complexity of the decoration that had been lavished on almost every item in the tomb.

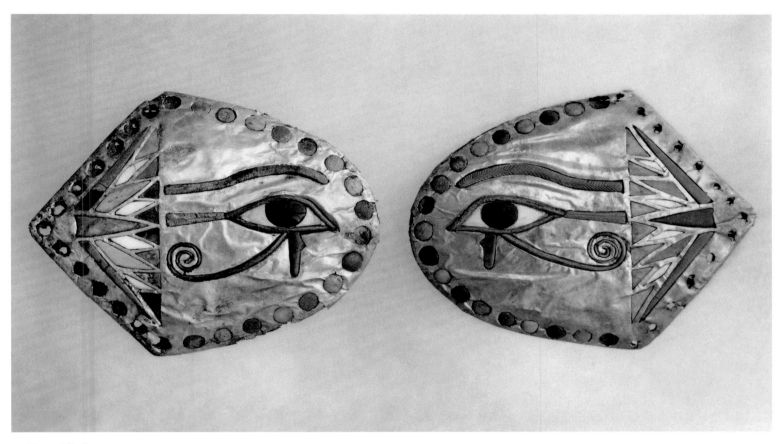

17. Horse blinders

Even objects as utilitarian as a pair of horse blinders were beautifully executed.

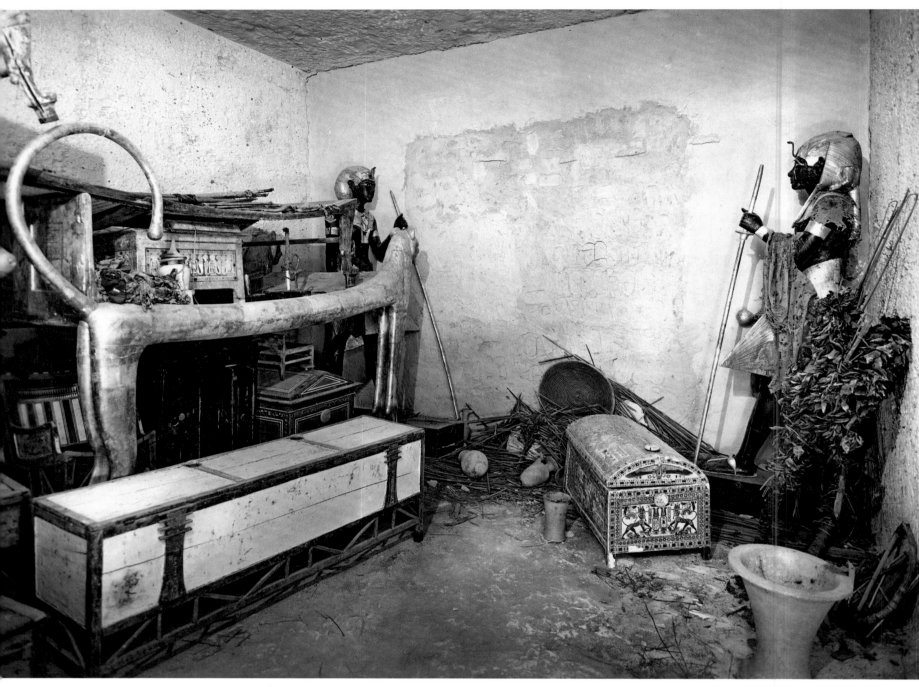

18. North wall of the Antechamber

At the far end of the Antechamber, in its north wall, was a third sealed (and resealed) doorway. It was flanked by two impressive life-size guardian statues of the king, covered in black resin and gilding. At the foot of one of the statues lay perhaps the most beautiful chest found in the tomb. Called the Painted Box, its sides are decorated with battle scenes of the young king triumphing over his enemies—here, the Syrians. This was the first object Carter removed from the tomb.

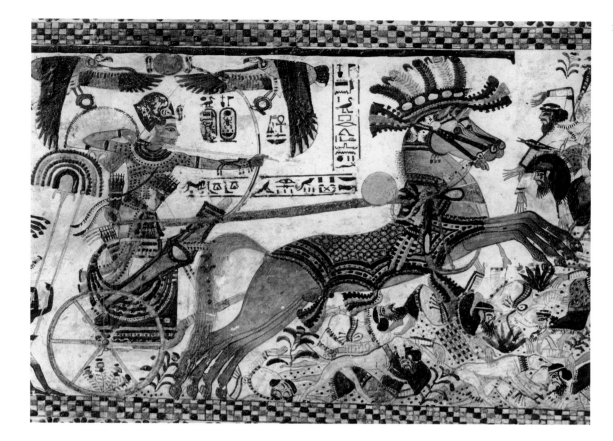

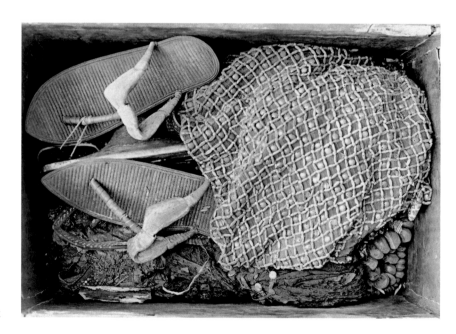

20. Contents of the Painted Box

What was such a splendid object meant to contain? Upon opening it, Carter found some of the king's clothing and sandals, including a heavily beaded garment that unfortunately disintegrated—as did nearly all of the textiles in the tomb.

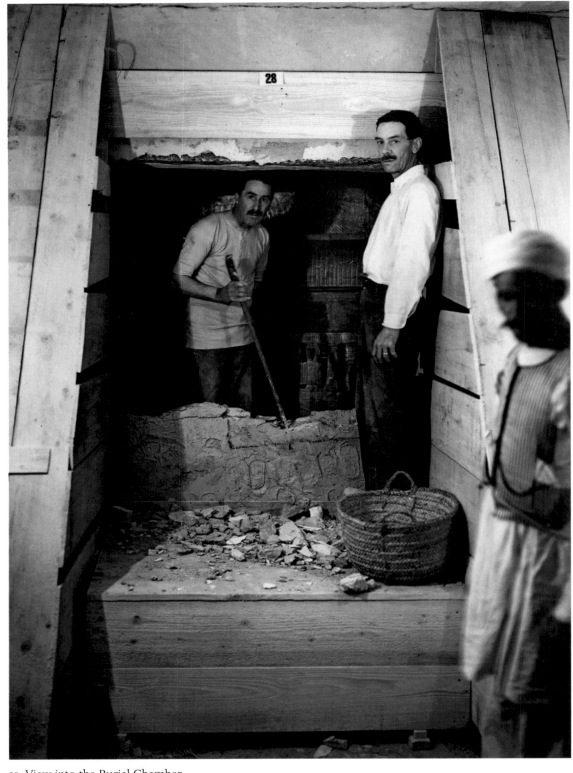

21. View into the Burial Chamber

Once the Antechamber was cleared, on February 17, 1923, Carter began carefully dismantling the third blocked doorway, removing it in sections so as to preserve the seal impressions in the mud plaster.

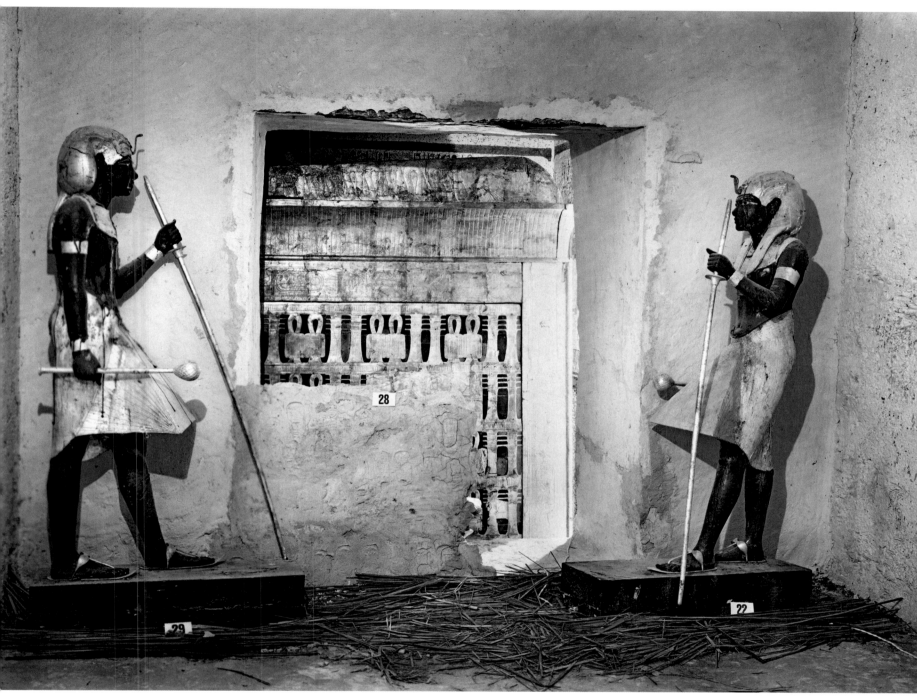

22. The partially unblocked doorway of the Burial Chamber

When the blocking between the Antechamber and the Burial Chamber was taken down, Carter found himself confronted by an almost solid wall of richly gilded wood—the south wall of the outermost shrine over the burial itself.

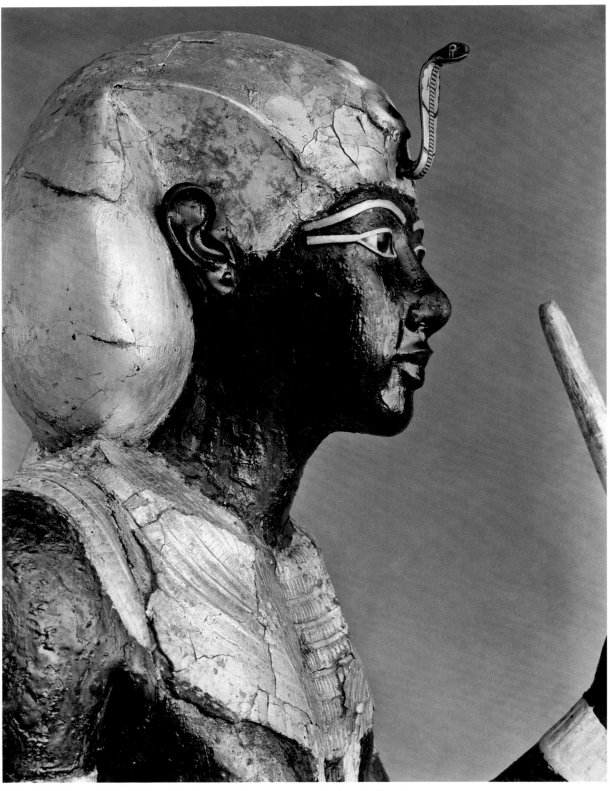

23. Detail of a guardian statue of the king at the entrance to the Burial Chamber

After the ceremonial opening of the Burial Chamber, Carter prepared for the removal of the guardian statues. They were heavily padded, and then secured to specially made carrying boxes with strips of cotton cloth.

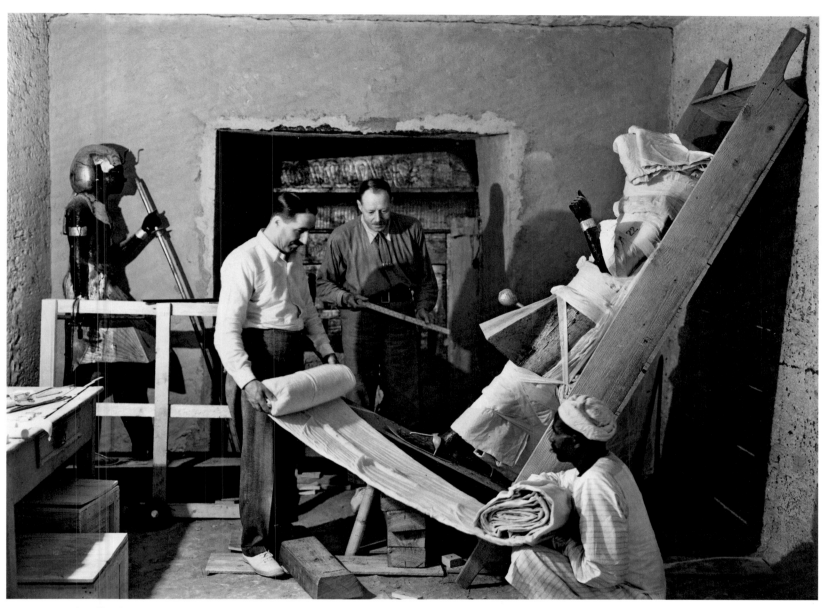

24. Carter and Callender wrap a guardian statue for removal from the tomb

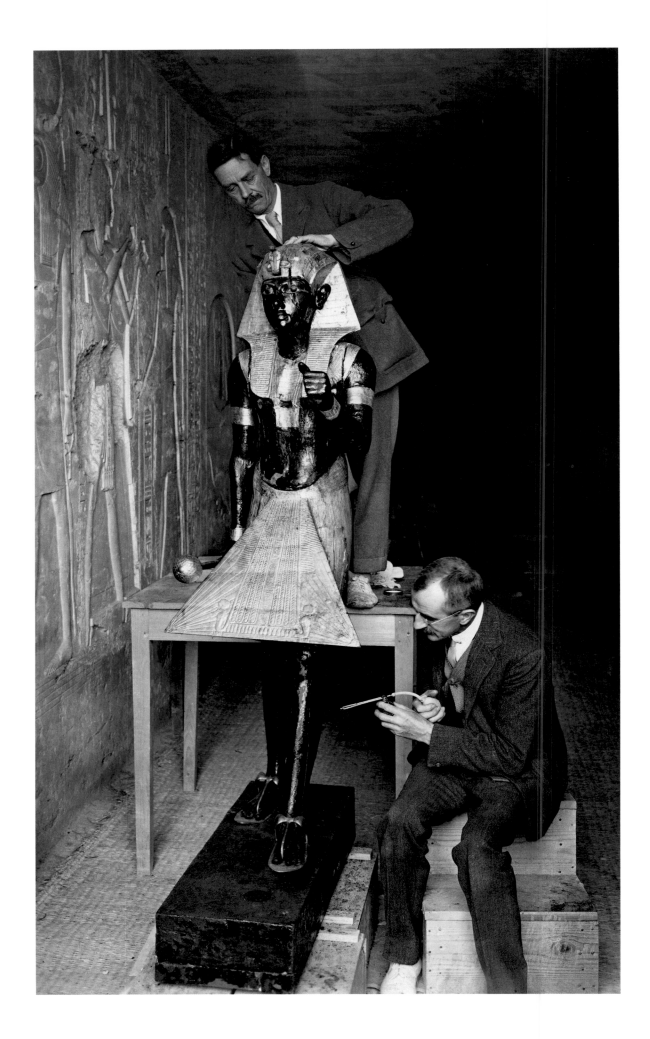

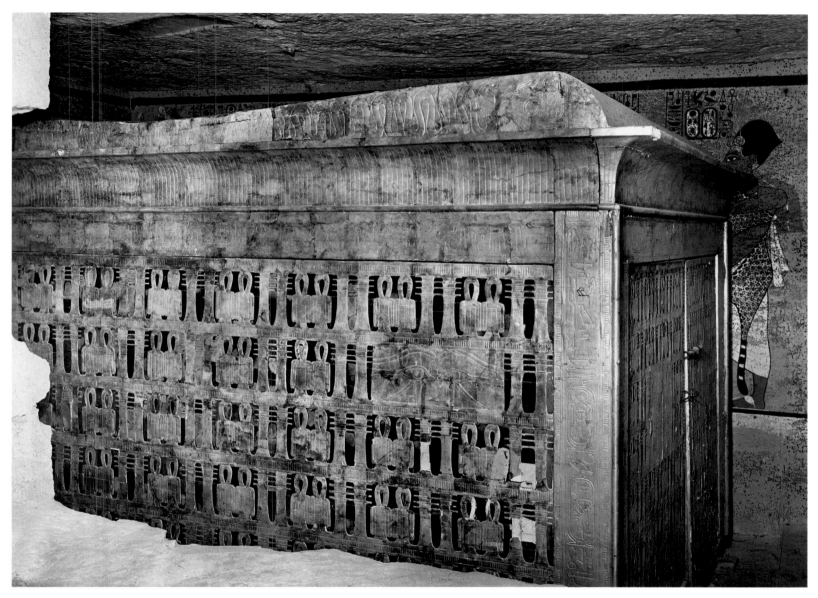

26. Outermost shrine in the Burial Chamber

Inside the Burial Chamber Carter was confronted by an enormous gilded wood shrine that nearly filled the space and left little room to maneuver. Clearly, the shrine—which now had to be taken apart—must have been put together in the chamber.

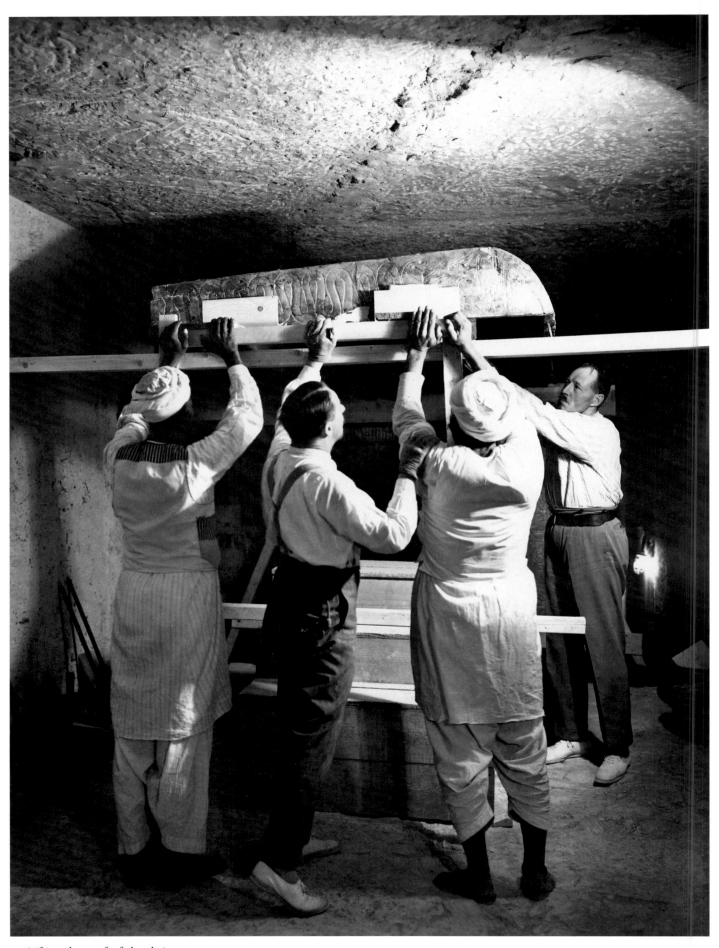

27. Lifting the roof of the shrine

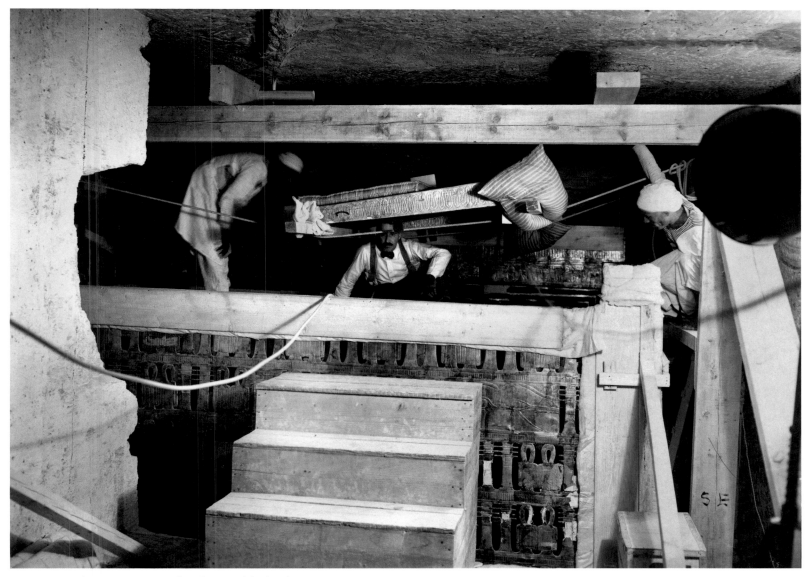

28. Beams and rigging were used to disassemble the shrines

Callender's engineering experience aided Carter in lighting the tomb and in rigging scaffolding and block and tackle in order to lift the roof of the shrine—a very difficult task, since the shrine itself took up nearly the entire Burial Chamber.

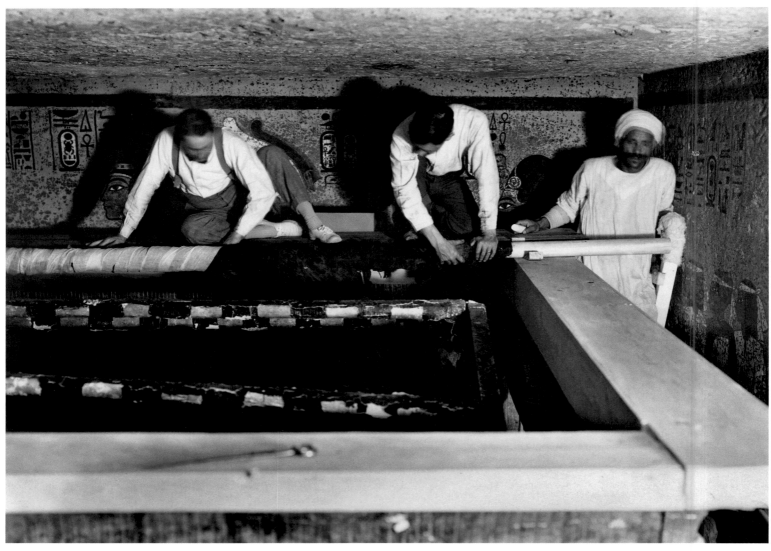
29. Removal of the fragile linen pall covering the shrine

When the roof of the outermost shrine had been removed, Carter must have been surprised to find, beneath it, a linen pall embroidered with heavy gilt-bronze rosettes, supported on a frame, underneath which was yet another shrine. The advanced state of decay of the delicate linen made it extremely difficult to handle it and to preserve it intact.

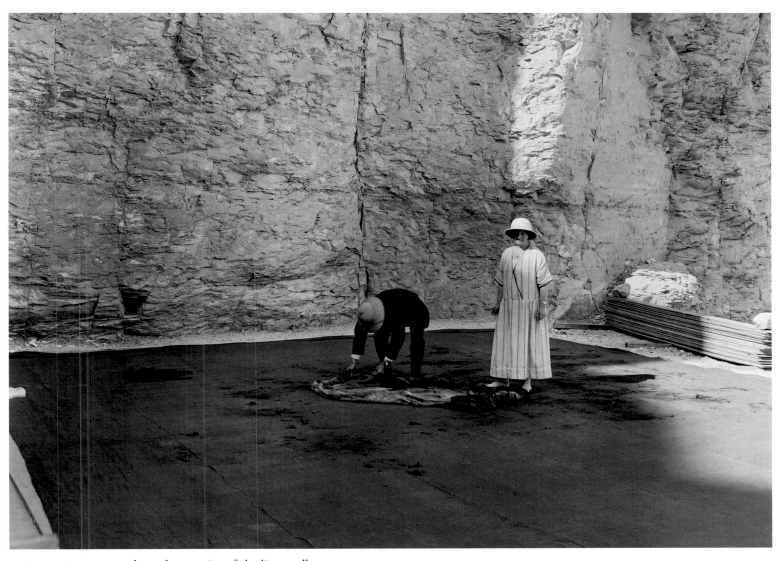

30. Attempting to spread out the remains of the linen pall

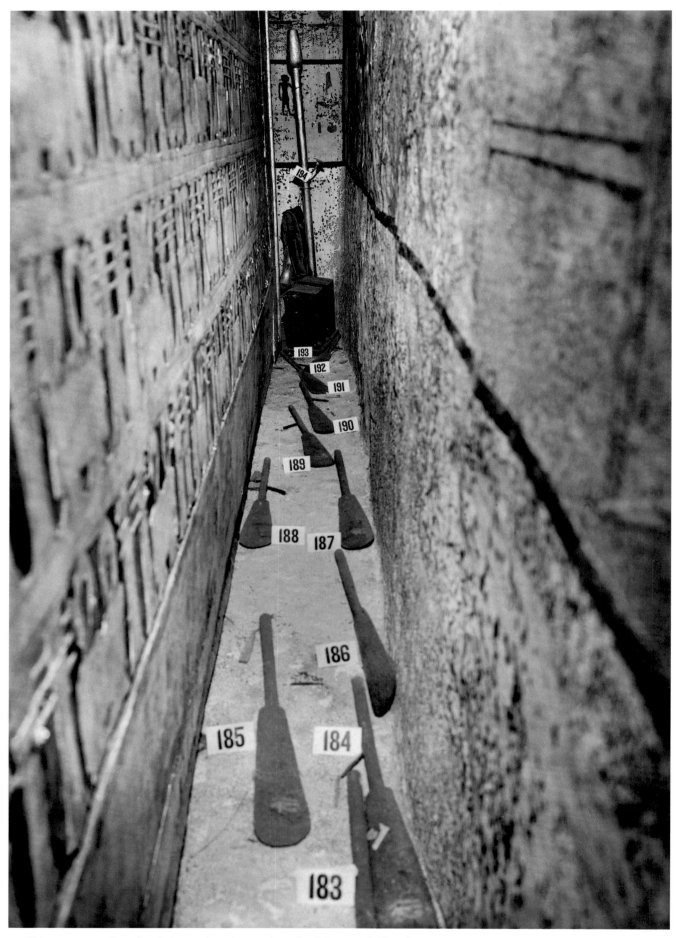

31. Objects surrounding the shrine against the north wall of the Burial Chamber

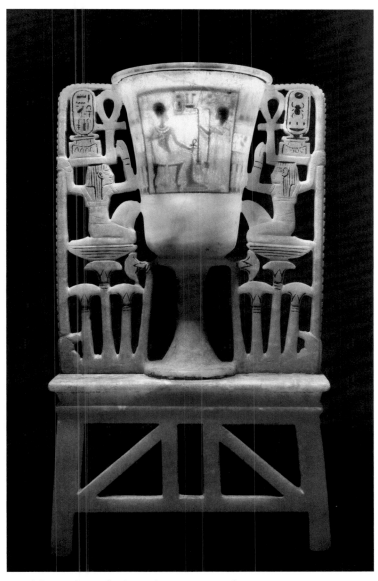

32. Alabaster lamp flanking the outermost shrine

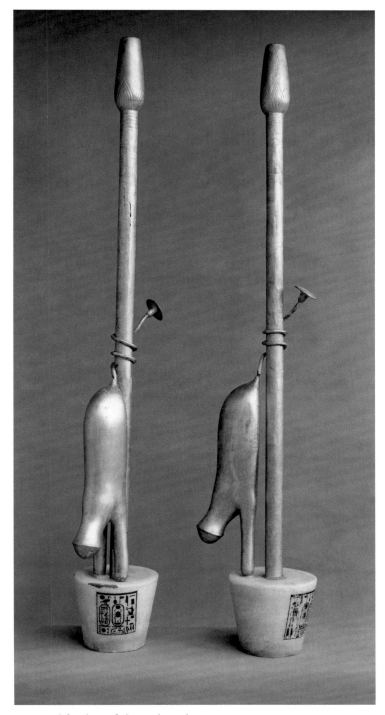

33. Wood fetishes of the god Anubis

Numerous objects—some of magical significance, such as oars, the divine fetishes of the god Anubis, and an alabaster lamp—had been carefully arranged around the outermost shrine, in the narrow space between the shrine and the tomb walls.

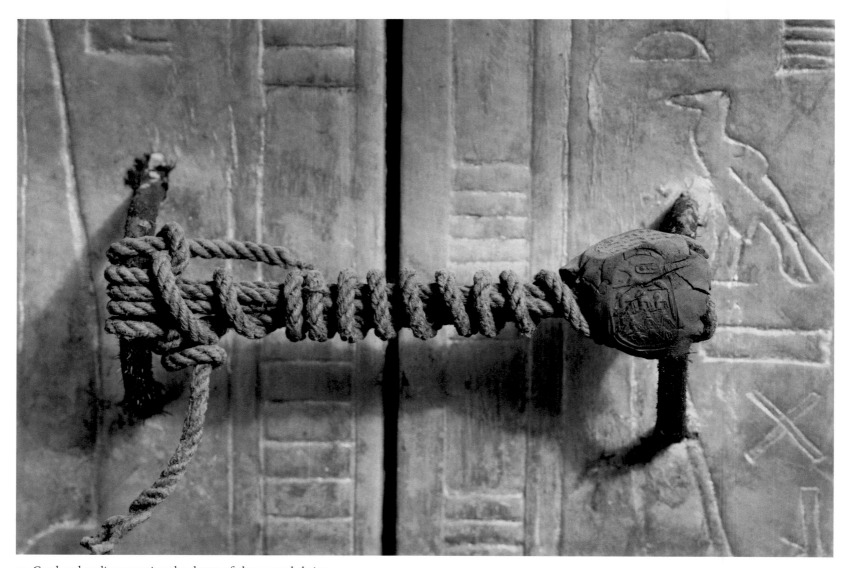

34. Cord and sealing securing the doors of the second shrine

Once the outermost shrine and the linen pall and frame had been removed, Carter saw that the second shrine remained secured with cord and a clay sealing impressed with the official seal of the necropolis. Hopes were raised that the burial within the shrine would be found intact.

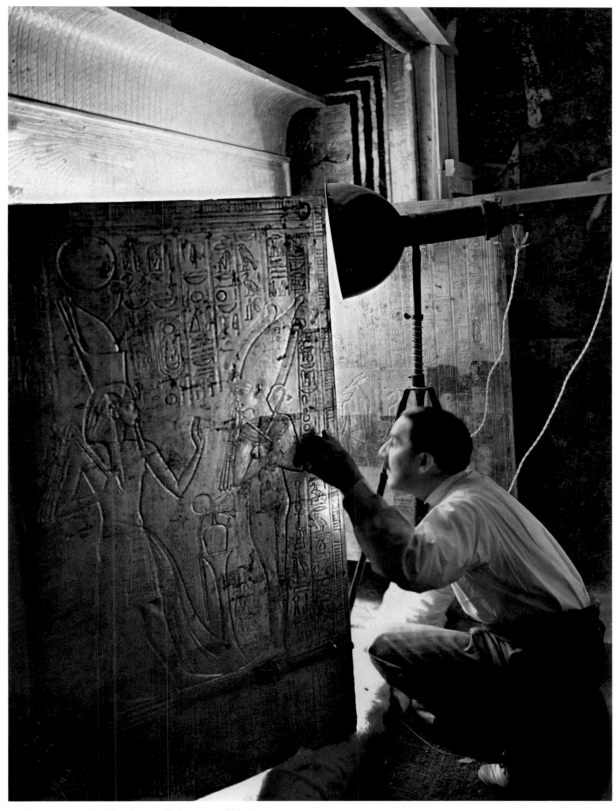

35. Carter opening the doors of the second shrine

Removing the seal, Carter opened the double doors of the shrine and peered in at the third of the four shrines over the sarcophagus. Dismantling all four shrines would take the team eight months.

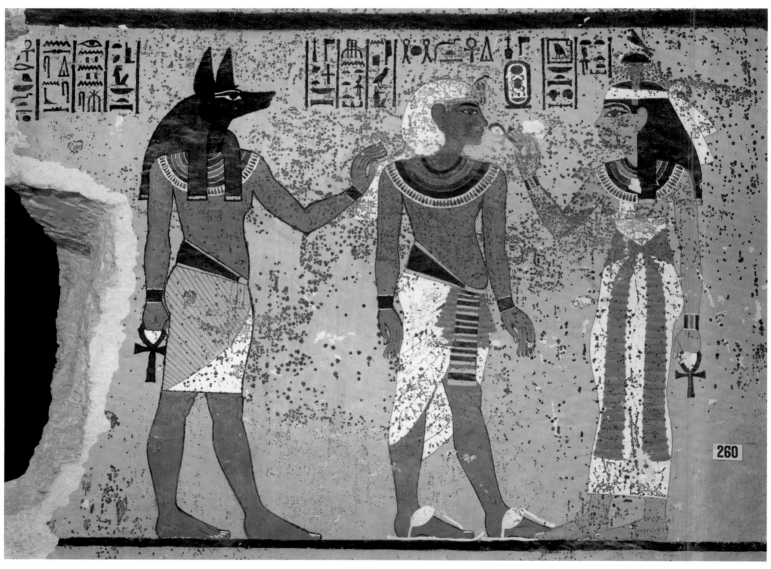

36. Painting on the south wall of the Burial Chamber

Once the four shrines were removed, the simple painted decoration of the Burial Chamber could be seen clearly. The funeral procession of the young king was depicted on one wall and on other walls he was shown in the presence of the gods.

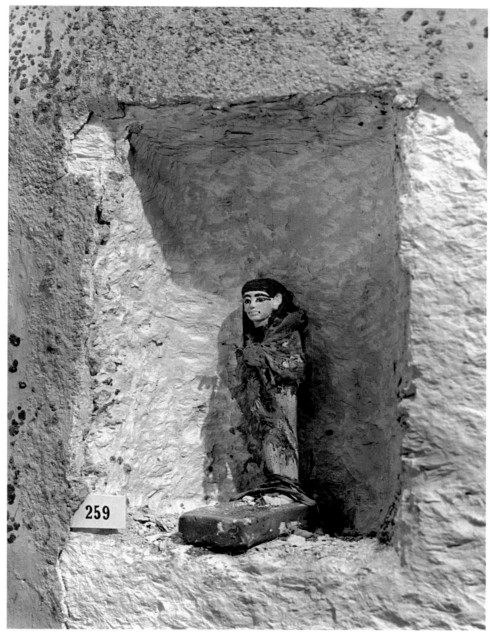

37. Painted figure in a niche in the Burial Chamber wall

Careful examination of the walls disclosed areas that appeared to have been replastered and painted over; when these sections were removed, four openings containing magic bricks and figures were revealed.

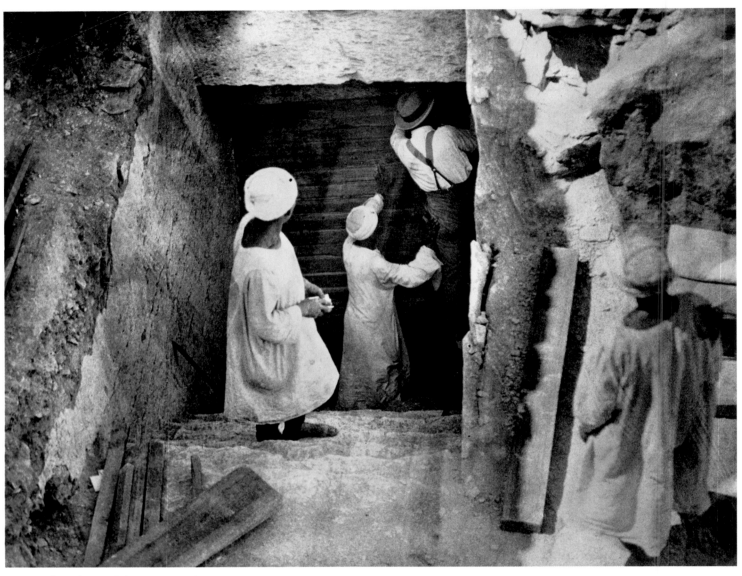

38. Resealing the tomb between working seasons

Since it was too hot to work in the Valley of the Kings in summer, at the end of each season the tomb had to be resealed and the staircase refilled for purposes of security.

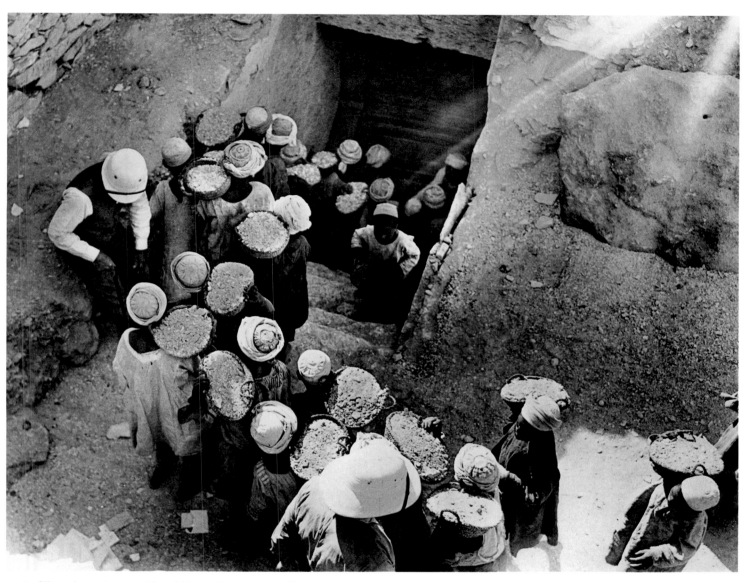

39. Refilling the stairway with rubble to deter grave robbers

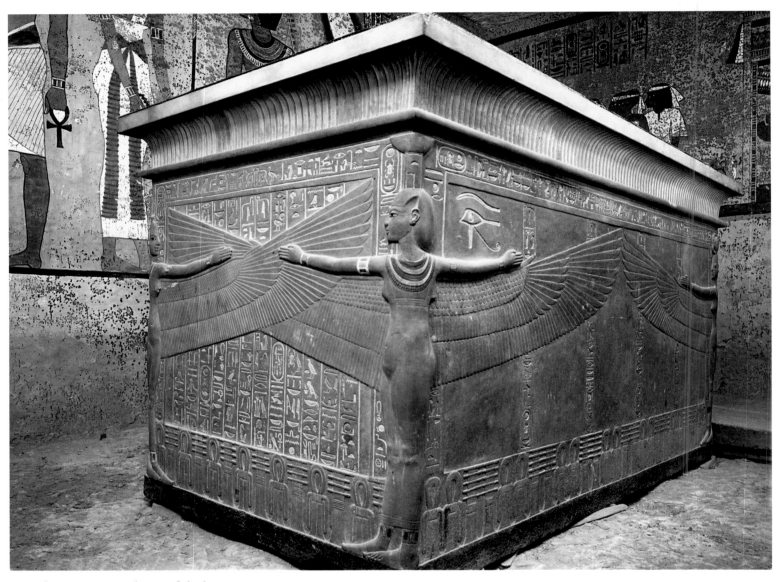

40. Red quartzite sarcophagus of the king

On February 12, 1924, Carter lifted the lid of the magnificent red quartzite sarcophagus that had been enclosed within the four shrines. Each corner was guarded by a winged goddess and inscribed with invocations to the gods to protect the king in the afterlife. Due to a dispute with the authorities about the work being carried out in the tomb, Carter ceased operations the next day and did not return until the following autumn.

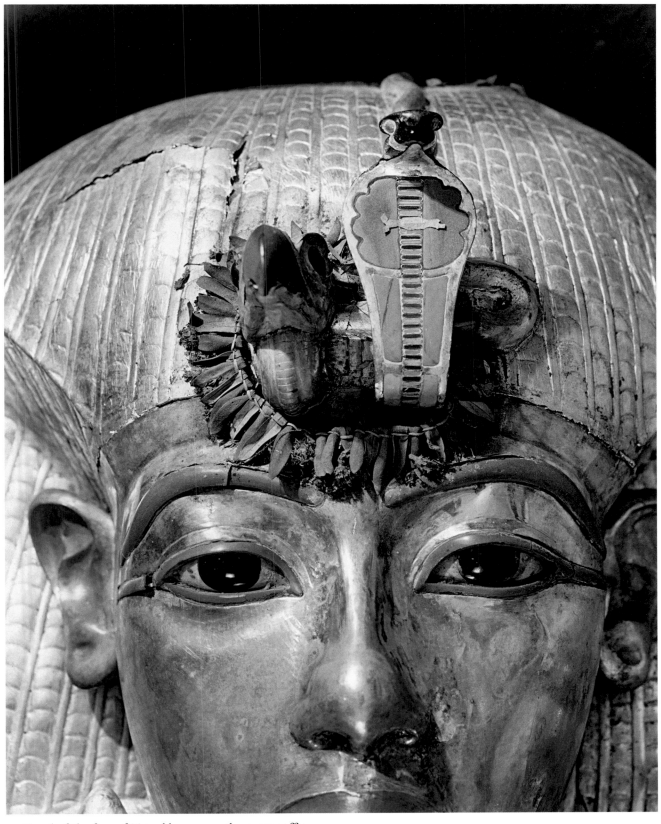

41. Detail of the face of Tutankhamun on the outer coffin

On October 13, 1925, Carter gazed upon the face of the first of three elaborately gilded and inlaid coffins. A small wreath of olive leaves and flowers was still intact around the royal uraeus on the pharaoh's brow.

42. Detail of the second coffin

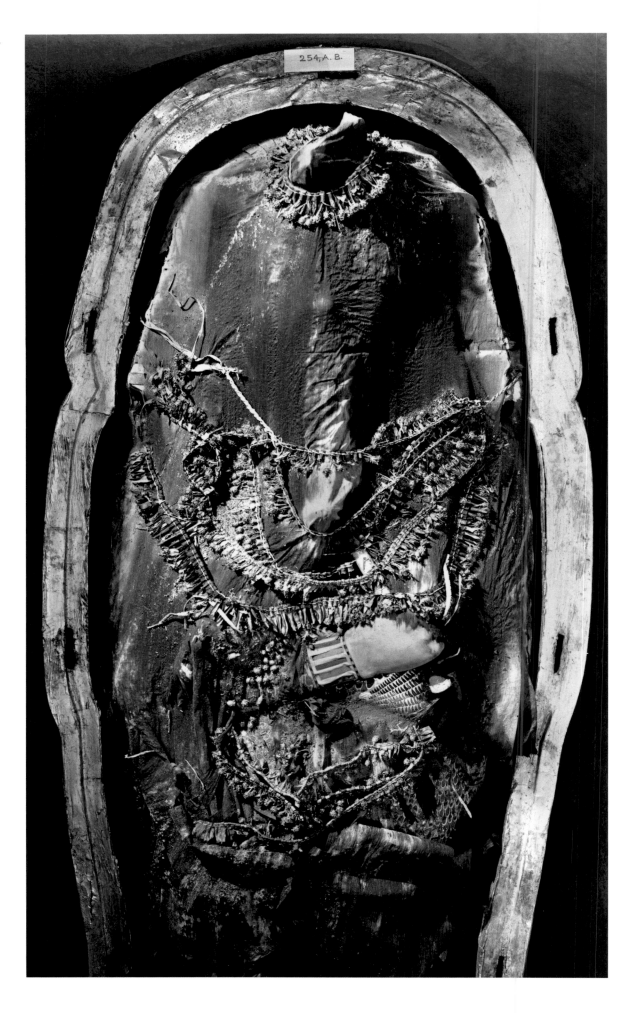

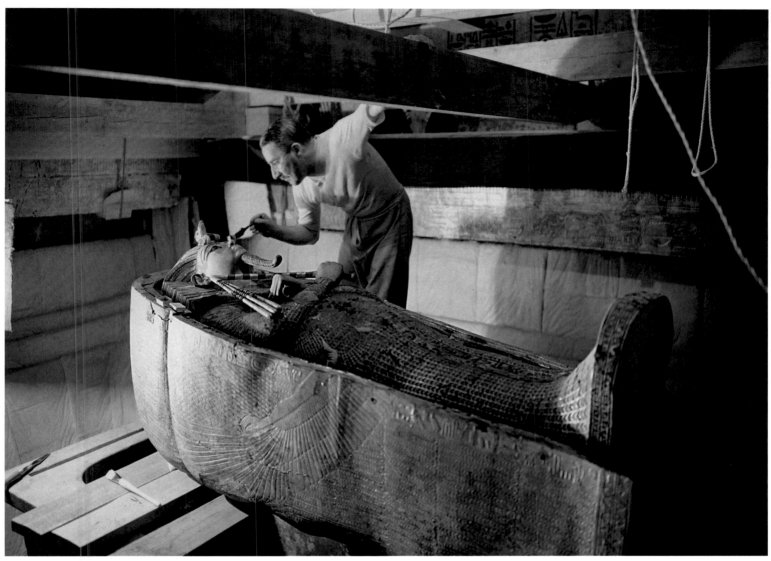

43. Carter cleans the second coffin

Removing the lid of the outer coffin, Carter found another coffin covered with a linen shroud and draped with floral garlands. Still uncertain of what lay within it, Carter lifted the extraordinarily heavy coffin out of the sarcophagus and slipped planks beneath it so that it could be examined more easily. When the lid of the second coffin was removed, the reason for the weight became apparent: the third, innermost coffin was made of solid gold.

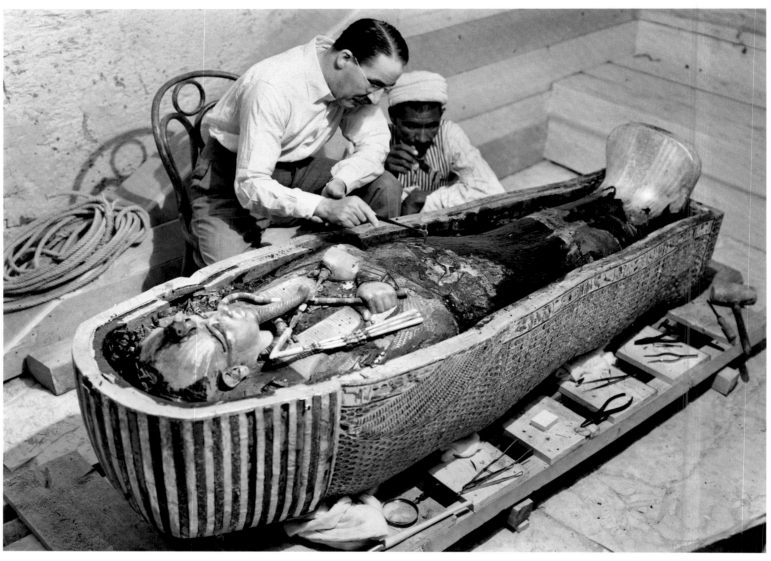

44. Carter examines the innermost gold coffin

Copious amounts of aromatic resin had been poured over the gold coffin and the mummy. These had solidified and darkened, so that the separation of the coffins required painstaking work. Within the gold coffin lay the mummy of Tutankhamun, his face covered by the now world-famous gold mask.

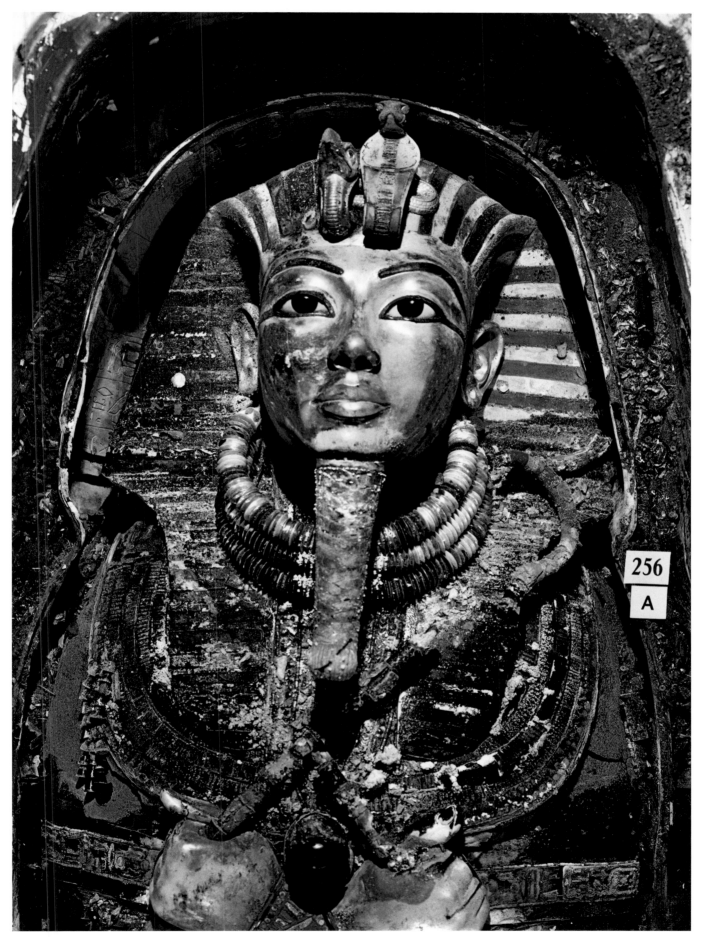

45. Gold mask of Tutankhamun

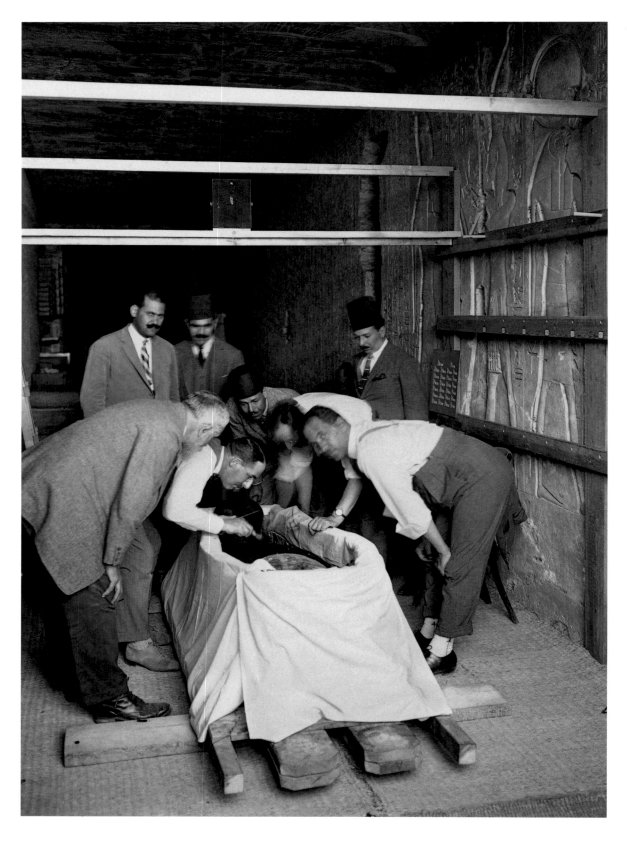

On November 11, 1929, the mummy finally was removed from the tomb and taken to the field laboratory
for examination by doctors and officials from the Egyptian Antiquities Service.

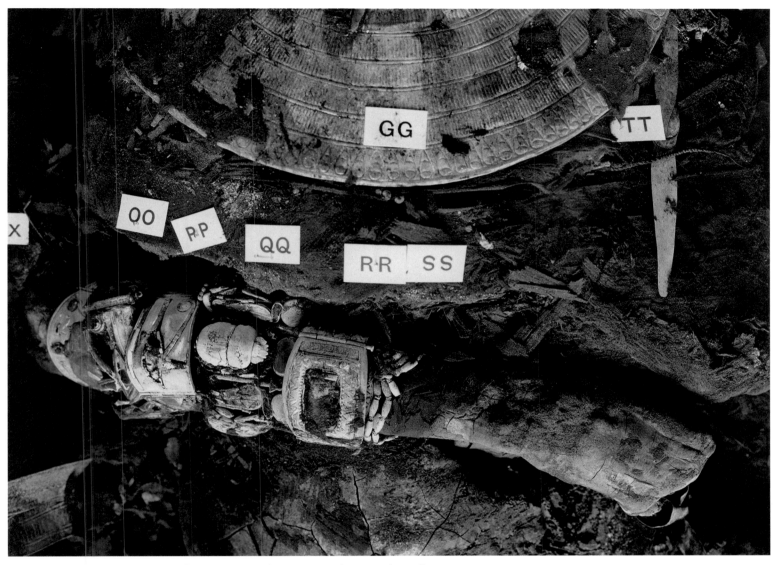

47. Detail of the chest and arms of the unwrapped mummy, with its jewelry still in position

As the unwrapping of the mummy proceeded, it was apparent that it had been badly damaged by the large amount of resins and ointments used in its preparation.

48. The thirteen bracelets found on the forearms of the mummy

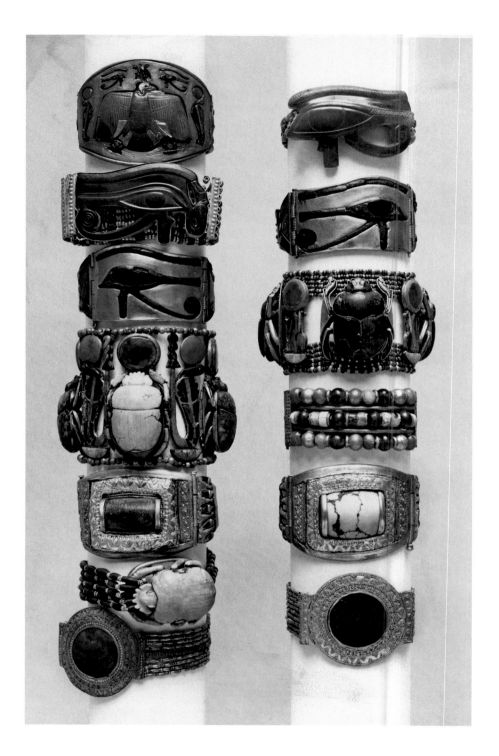

In death, the king had been adorned with many pieces of magnificent jewelry, such as these thirteen bracelets, which covered each arm from wrist to elbow.

Having cleared the Antechamber and the Burial Chamber, Carter turned his attention to the adjacent Treasury on October 24, 1926, where the canopic shrine housing the king's internal organs was located. It was guarded by a figure of the jackal god Anubis on top of a portable shrine.

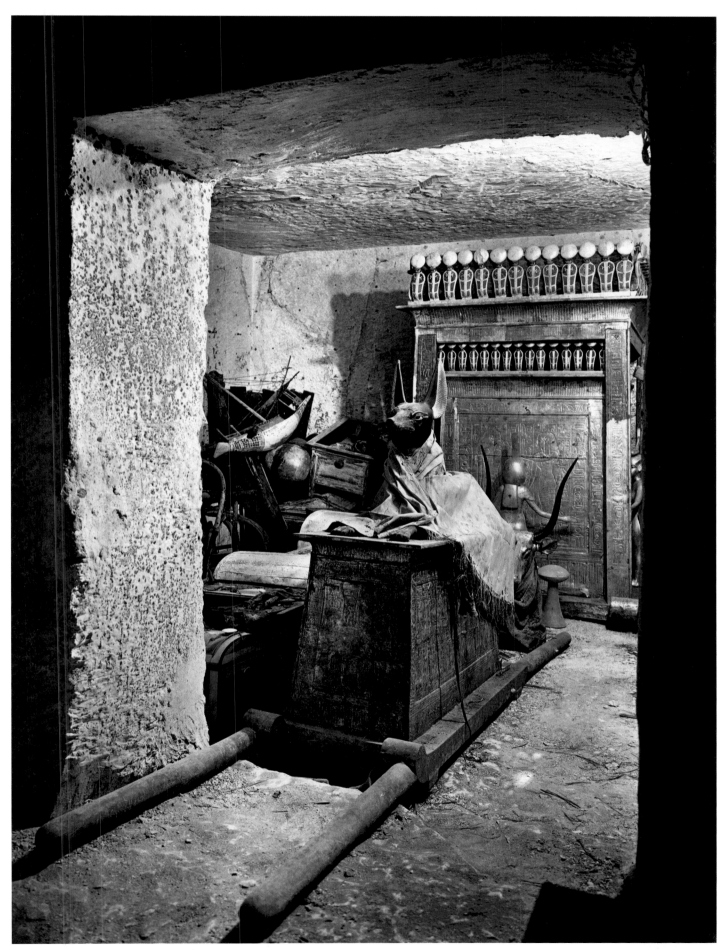

49. The Treasury entrance, guarded by a statue of the god Anubis atop a shrine

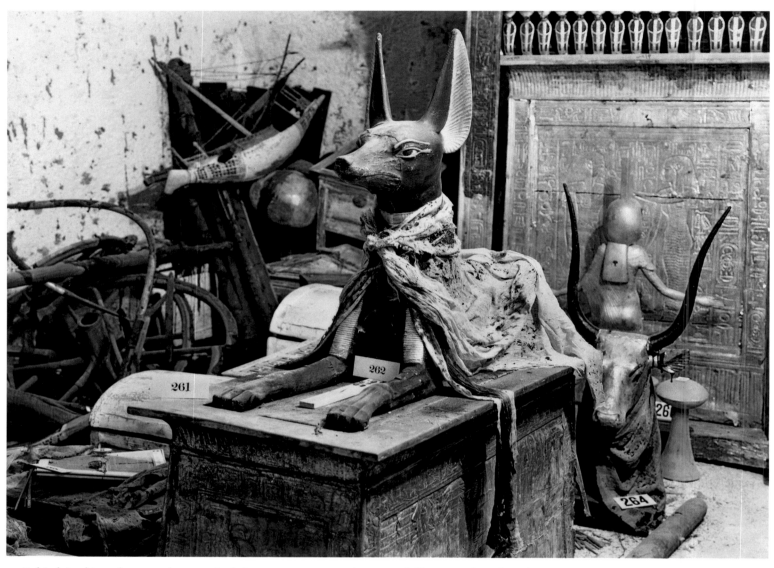

50. Behind Anubis and next to the canopic shrine were numerous chests, model boats, and another chariot

The figure of Anubis, draped in a fringed linen tunic, had streamers tied around its neck. Had it been carried in the funeral procession?

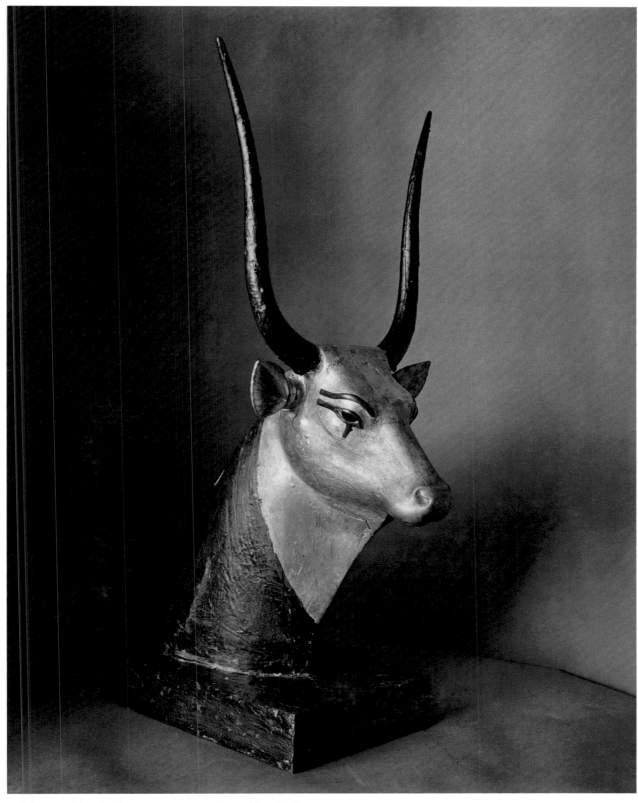

51. The wood head of a cow represents the goddess Hathor

Behind Anubis, on the floor in front of the canopic shrine, stood a gilded wood head of Hathor, Mistress of the West—and, therefore, also of the necropolis—in the form of a cow.

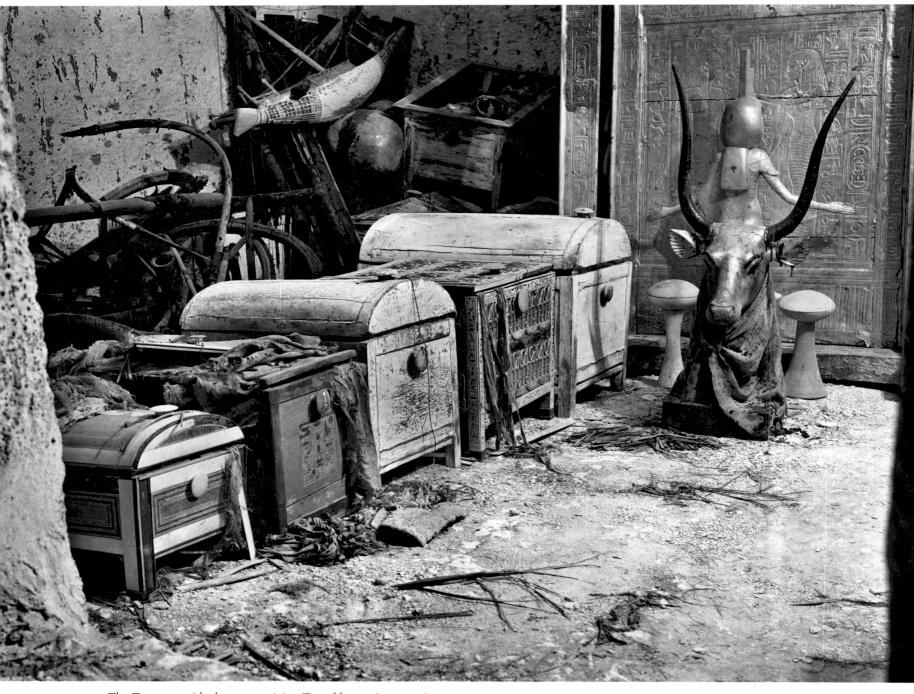

52. The Treasury, with chests containing Tutankhamun's possessions

Also on the floor of the Treasury were several elaborately made boxes, or caskets; originally sealed, they clearly had been opened and rifled by thieves.

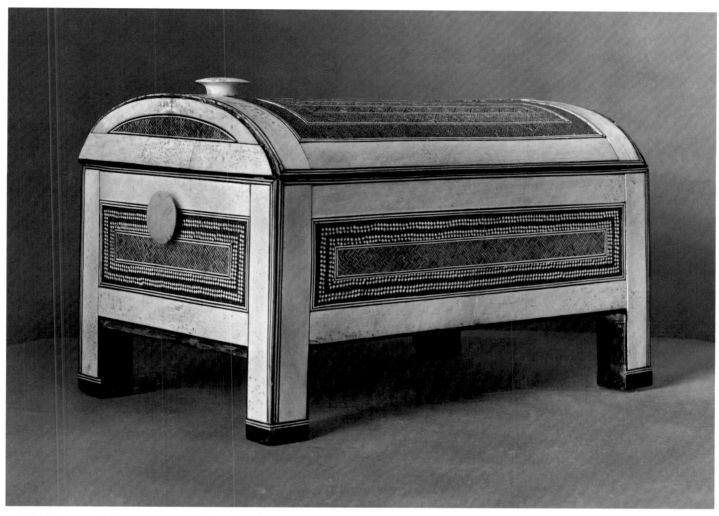

53. Inlaid ivory-and-ebony marquetry chest found in the Treasury

Each box was the work of a master craftsman. One of the most astonishing examples was inlaid with more than forty-seven thousand pieces of ivory and ebony, according to Carter's estimate. The ink inscription on the lid noted that the box contained jewelry to be worn by the king in official processions.

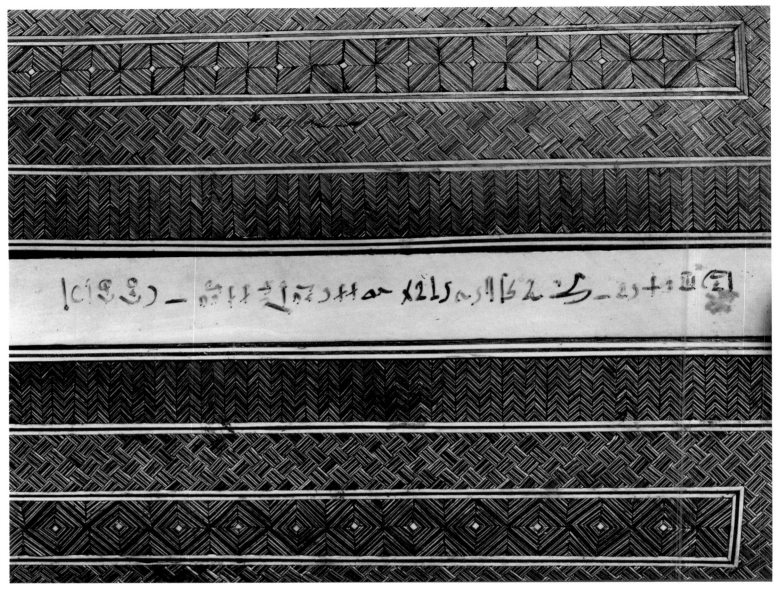

54. An inscription on the lid notes that the marquetry chest held the king's jewelry

When the chest was opened, Carter found a jumble of jewelry and other objects inside, including two beautiful pectorals of gold and semiprecious stones.

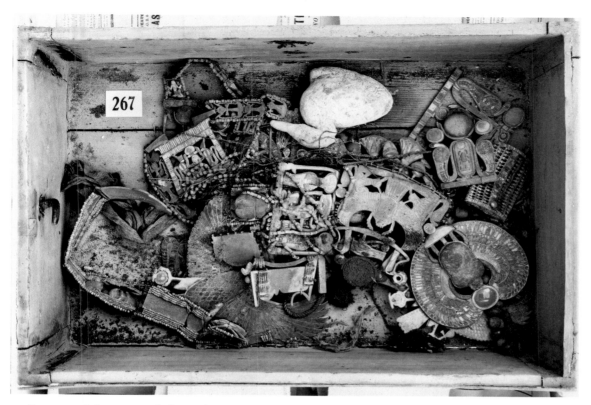

55. Contents of the ivory-and-ebony chest

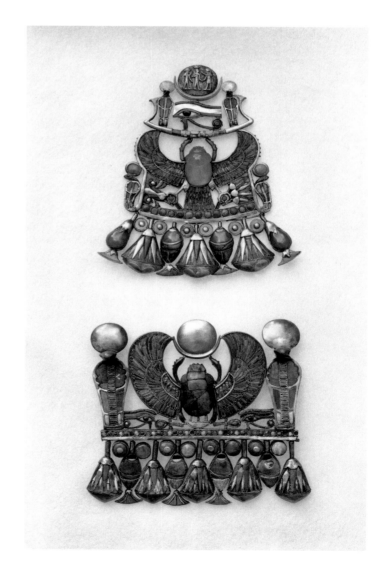

56. Gold and jeweled pectorals from the inlaid chest

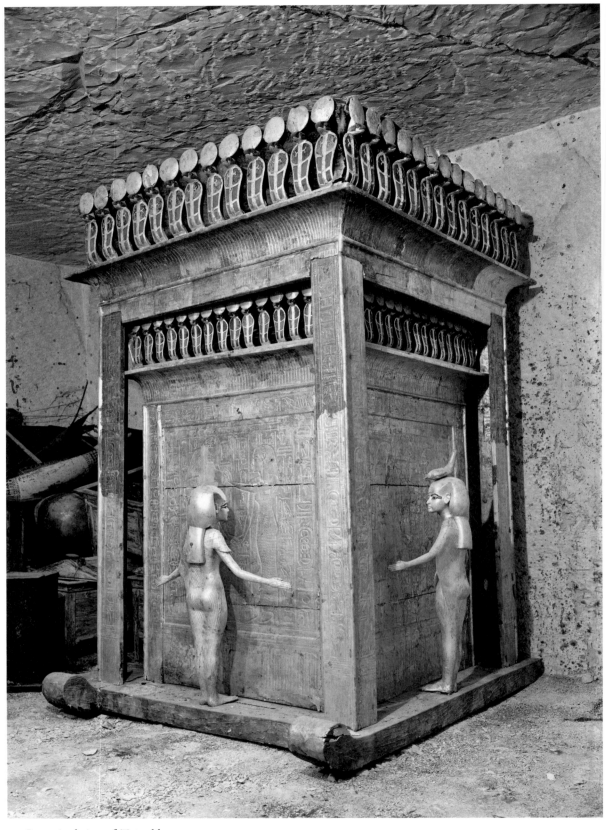

57. Canopic shrine of Tutankhamun

Once the figures and caskets in front of it had been cleared away, the canopic shrine itself could be examined more closely. A massive gilded box crowned by an elaborate cornice and placed on a sled, each of its sides was guarded by one of the tutelary goddesses—Isis, Nepthys, Neith, and Selket.

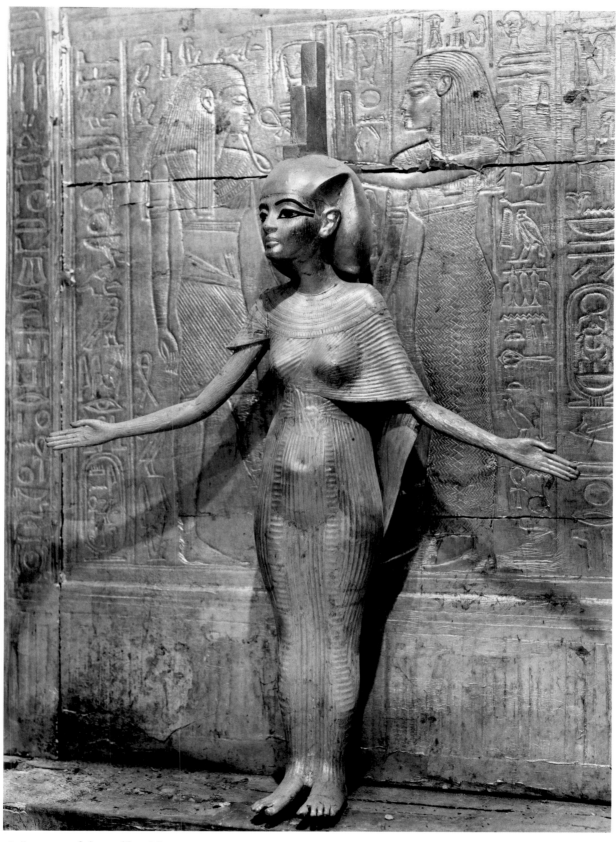

58. Statuette of the goddess Isis

Each goddess was dressed in a sheer, delicately pleated linen robe, her head covered with a bag wig surmounted by her emblem; the emblem of Isis, for example, is a throne. Like the shrine, the figures were gilded and painted.

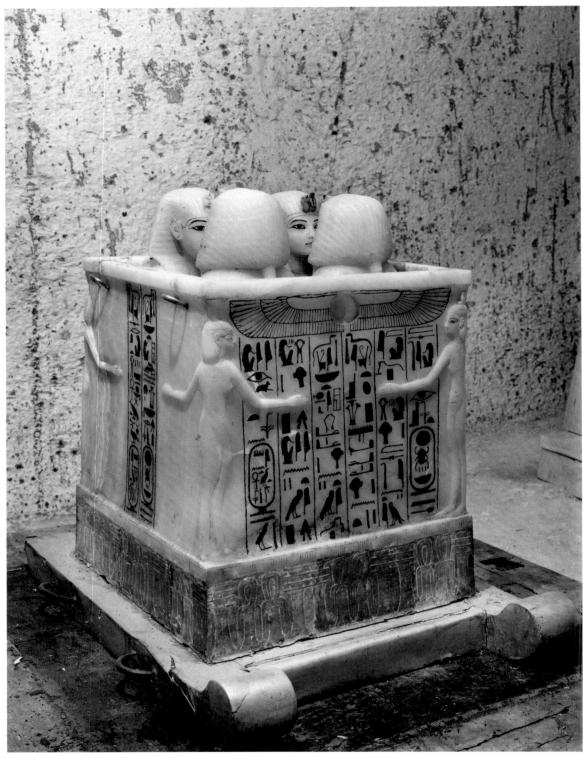

59. The alabaster canopic chest, discovered within the outer canopic shrine

Beneath the outer shrine was an alabaster canopic chest. Again, the four tutelary goddesses guarded each corner, as they had on the quartzite sarcophagus. Carter removed the heavy stone lid, revealing four heads of the king, which served as the closures of the compartments containing his mummified internal organs.

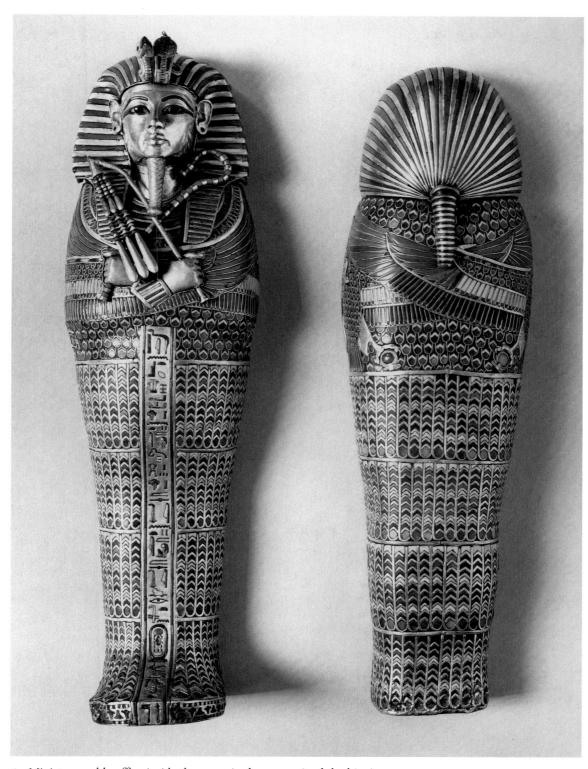

60. Miniature gold coffins inside the canopic chest contained the king's organs

Within each of these compartments was an exquisite miniature gold coffin for the mummified bundles: that of Imseti, protected by Isis, held the king's liver.

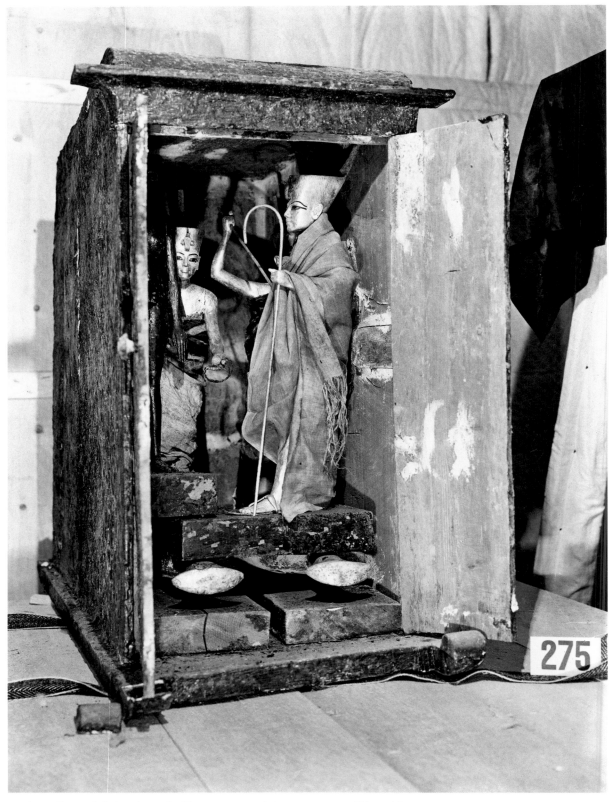

61. A small wood shrine from the Treasury, containing statuettes of Tutankhamun

Also found in the Treasury were many darkly varnished wood shrines with double doors, which housed small statues of the king and the gods, each figure garbed for eternity in a cloak of linen.

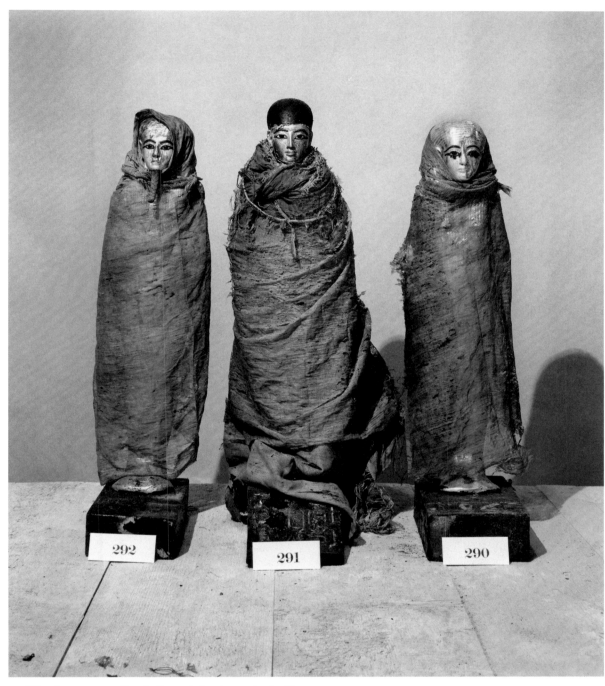

62. Wood statuettes of gods from shrine boxes in the Treasury

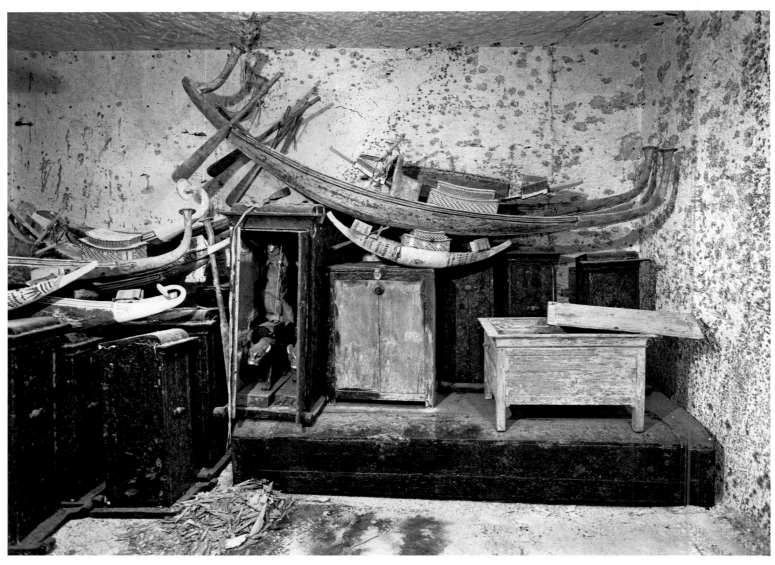

63. Wood shrines with statuettes, and large models of boats, found in the Treasury

On top of the shrines were eighteen large, colorfully painted wood boats symbolically ready for the king to use on his journeys in the afterlife.

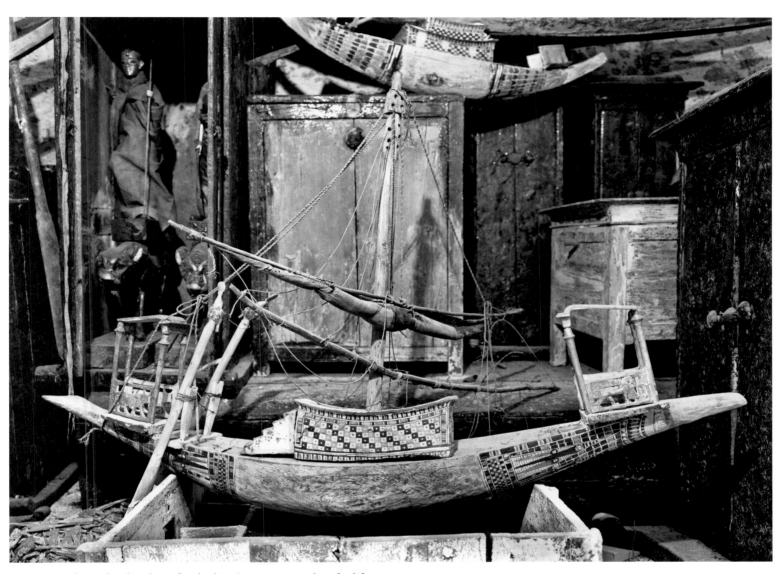

64. A painted wood sailing boat for the king's journeys in the afterlife

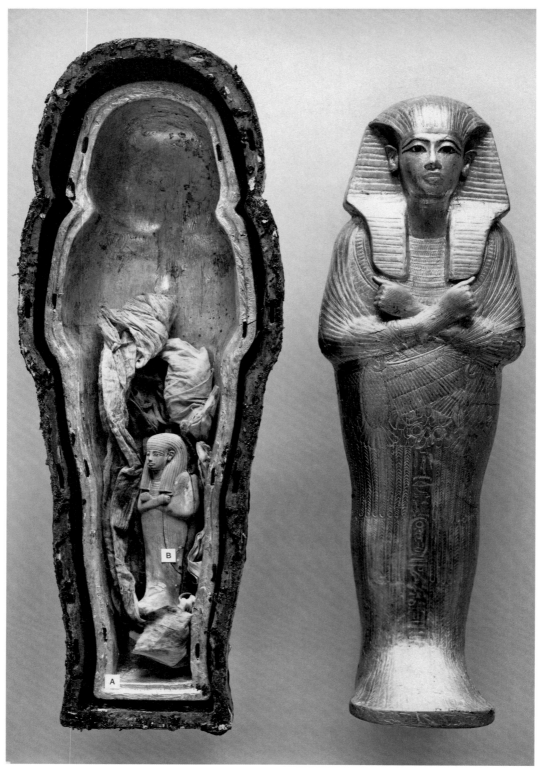

65. Gilded miniature nested coffins from the Treasury held jewelry and a lock of hair

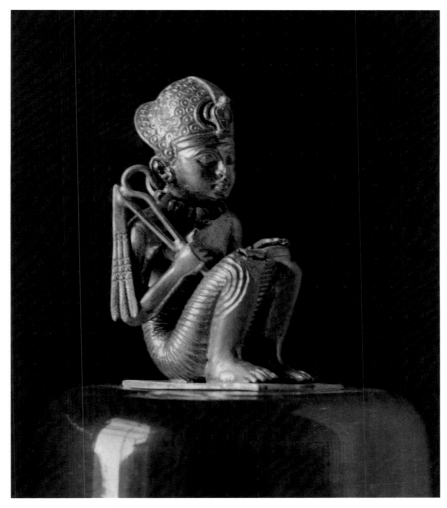

66. Gold amulet of the king represented as a squatting child

It appeared that many of the items placed in the Treasury were those most important to Tutankhamun, either personally or magically. A small set of gilded miniature nested coffins held a lock of the hair of Queen Tiye, wife of Amenhotep III, who was probably Tutankhamun's grandmother, as well as a unique, solid-gold amulet of the king, only two inches high, in the form of a squatting child.

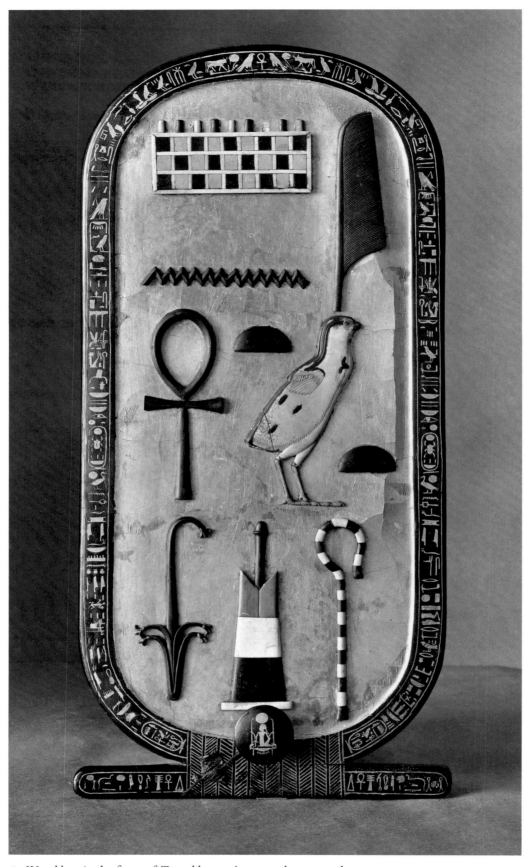

67. Wood box in the form of Tutankhamun's cartouche, or royal name

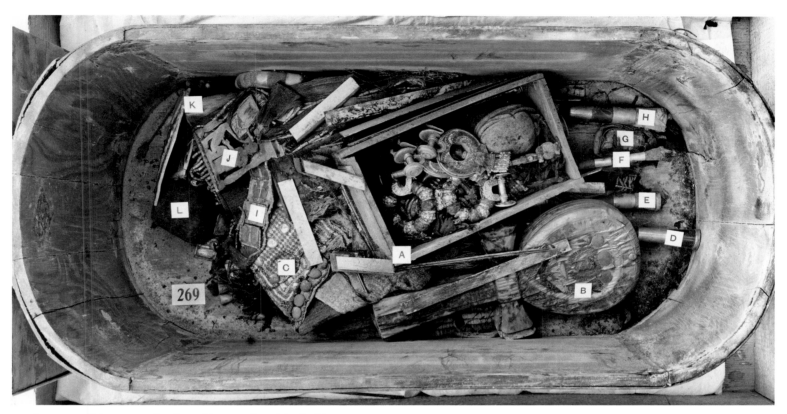

68. Contents of the cartouche-shaped box, as found in the Treasury

As each box was opened, the excavators invariably were surprised by what they found, although the objects often had been broken and jumbled together by the tomb robbers. This box, which is in the form of the king's cartouche, or royal name, contained a beautiful lunar pectoral and two pairs of scepters and flails—the royal insignia that a pharaoh held crossed in front of his chest.

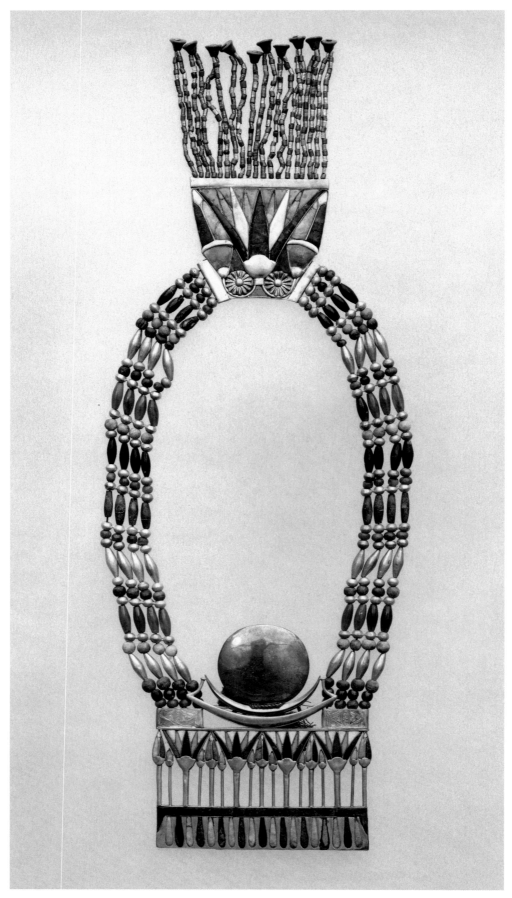

69. Tutankhamun's necklace, discovered in the cartouche box

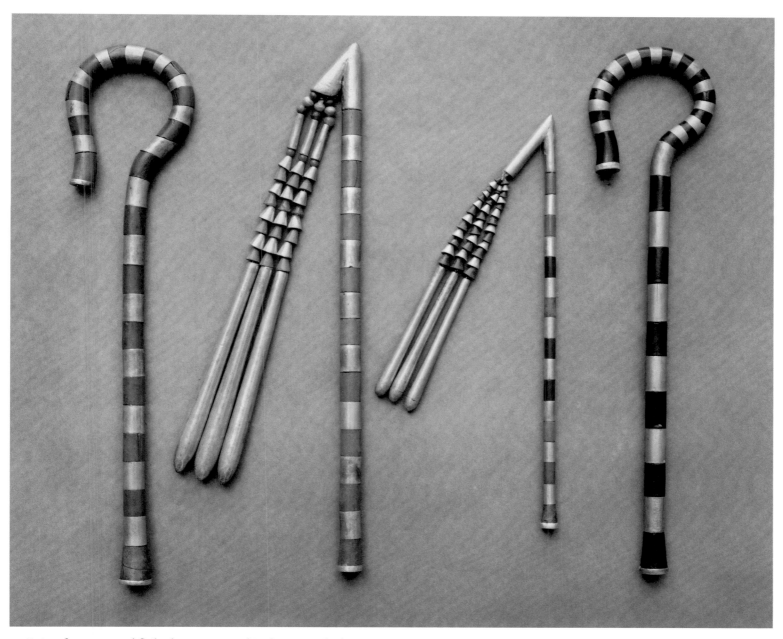

70. Pairs of scepters and flails also were stored in the cartouche box

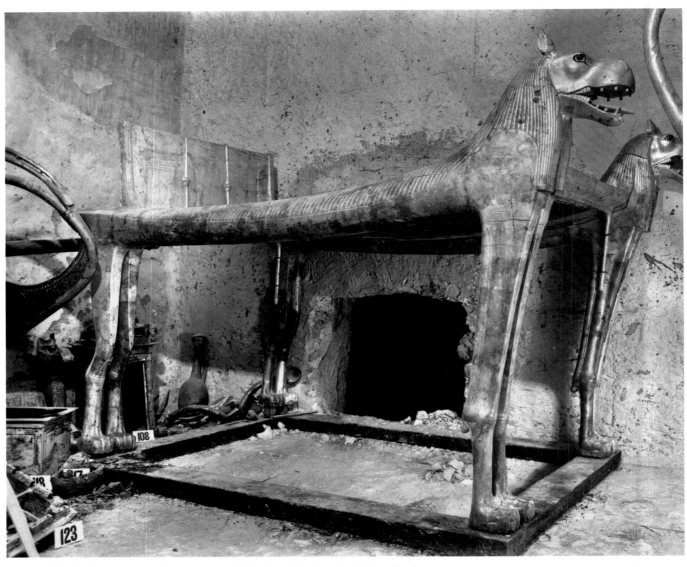

71. An unblocked opening in the west wall of the Antechamber leads into the Annex

The Annex was the last room in the tomb to which Carter and his team turned their attention. Entered through a small opening behind one of the animal-headed ritual couches, it, too, had been discovered and invaded by the tomb robbers.

72. (Opposite): Detail of the hippopotamus goddess from a ritual couch in the Antechamber

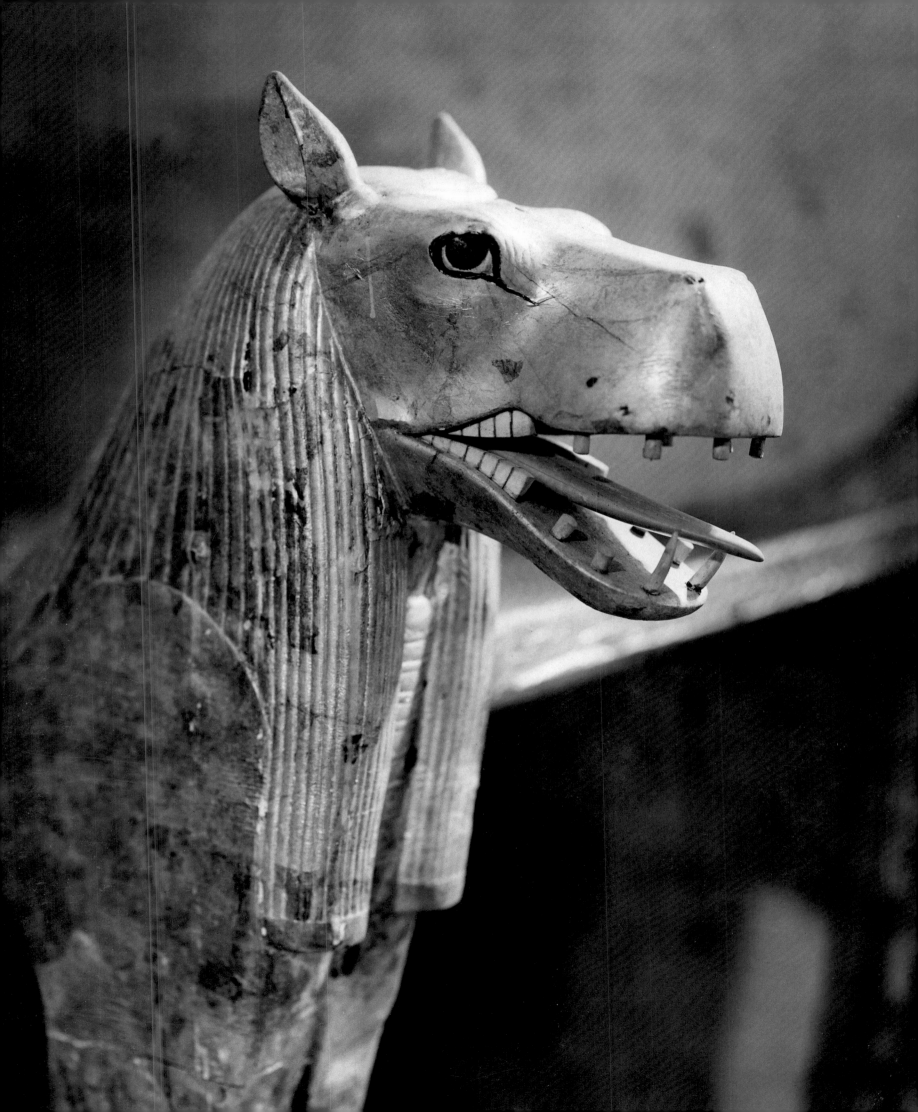

73. Furniture, boxes, baskets, pottery jars, and stone vessels crowded the Annex

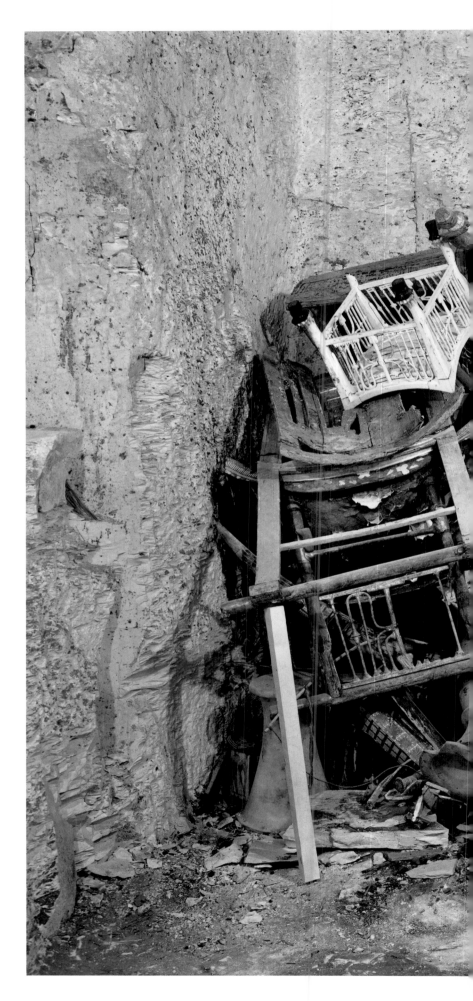

The narrow Annex was heaped with furniture, vessels, and baskets—in places, almost five feet high. Originally intended as a storage room for provisions, the Annex also contained items that should have been put in the Antechamber and the Treasury. In total more than two thousand individual objects were found in the Annex, and it took some six weeks to empty the chamber of its contents.

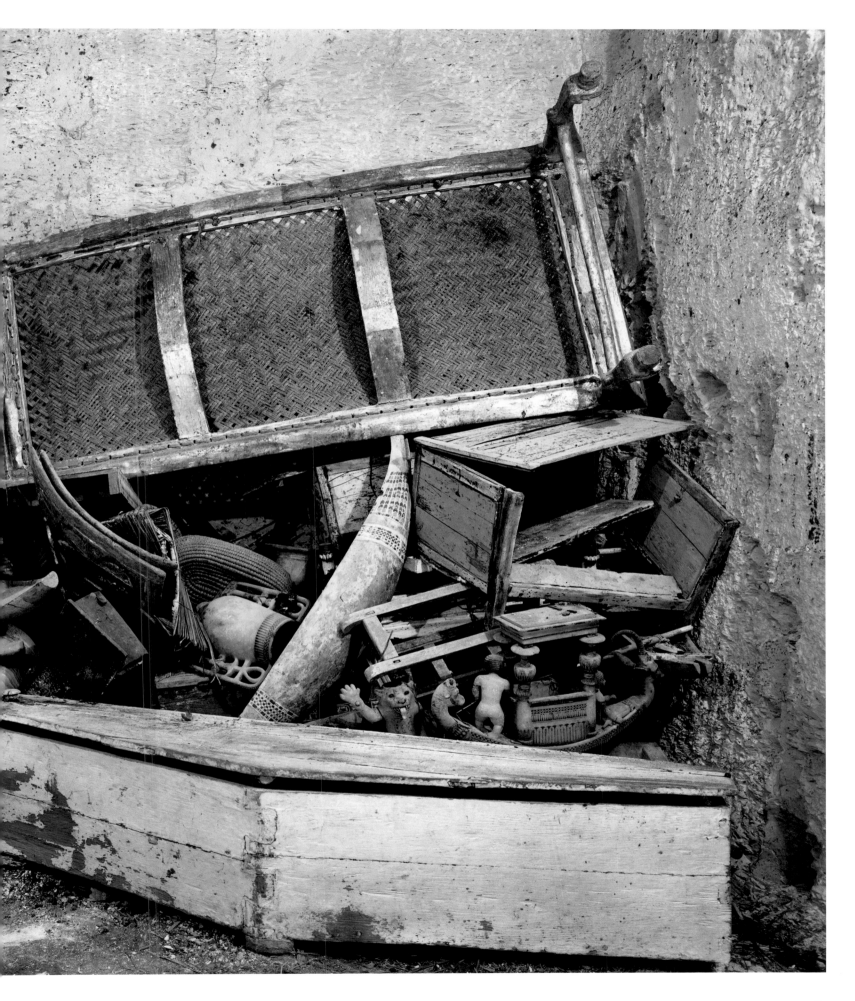

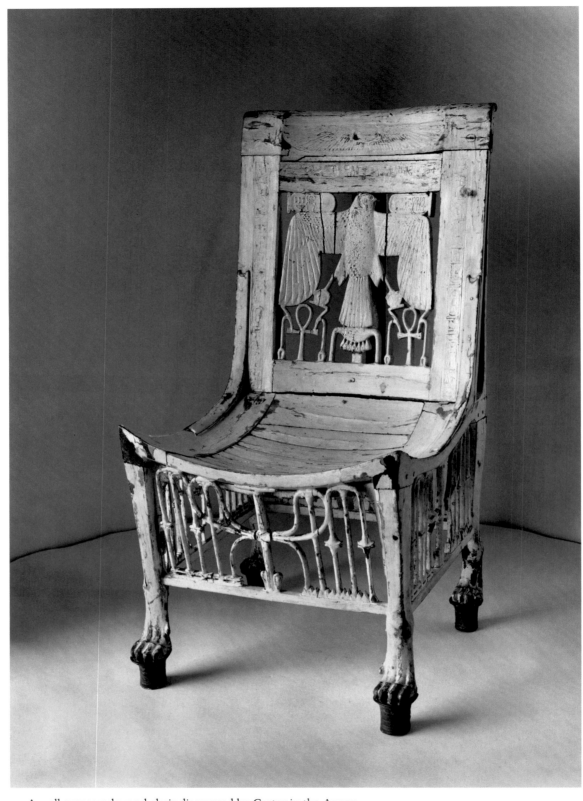

74. A well-preserved wood chair discovered by Carter in the Annex

Carefully disentangling the pile of items, Carter found this carved-and-painted wood chair, or throne.

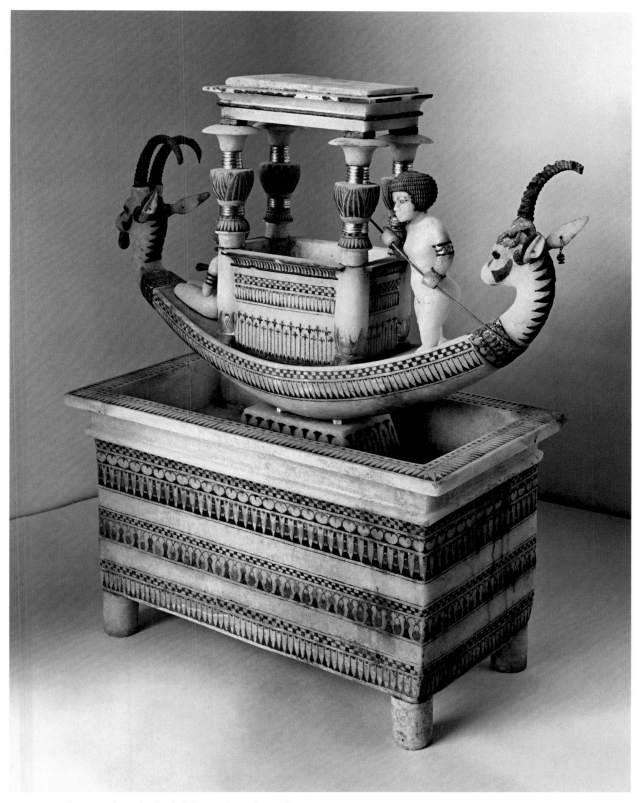

75. A carved, painted, and inlaid alabaster boat from the Annex

Remarkably crafted objects were found in the Annex as well, such as an alabaster boat steered by a dwarf, which was placed upon a pedestal meant to indicate a pond. Carter believed that the boat was probably an elaborate centerpiece intended to hold flowers at a banquet.

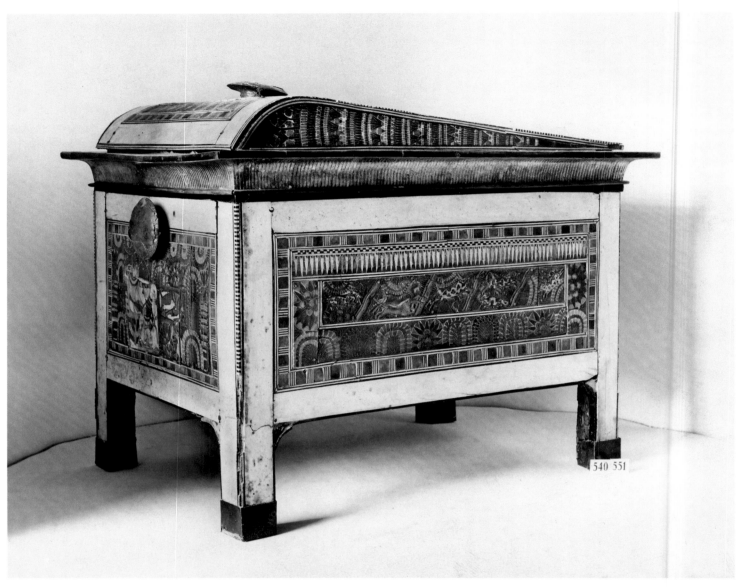

76. A wood-and ivory shrine-like box from the Annex

As in the other parts of the tomb, elaborately and lavishly decorated caskets and chests were discovered in the Annex. One example, inlaid with ivory, has become famous for the intimate scene of Tutankhamun and his wife, Ankhesenamun, on its lid.

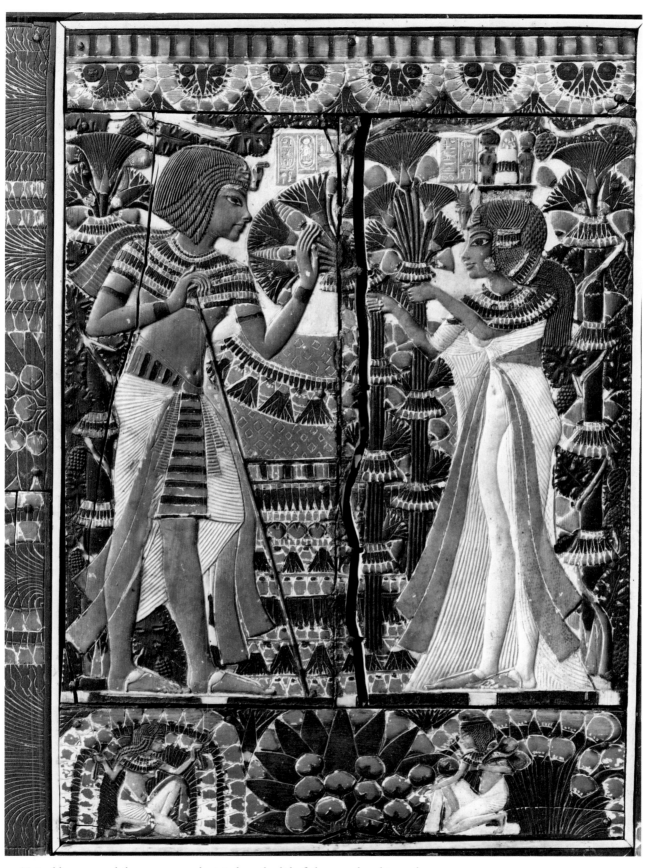

77. Tutankhamun and the queen are depicted on the lid of the wood-and-ivory box

On November 10, 1930, the last objects buried with Tutankhamun were removed from the tomb. Conservation of the finds continued until the spring of 1932, when the final shipment was sent to the Egyptian Museum in Cairo. Almost a quarter of a century had passed since Howard Carter and Lord Carnarvon first began their search for Tutankhamun's tomb. The body of Tutankhamun, in his second coffin, remains to this day in his sarcophagus in his tomb in the Valley of the Kings.

The goal of every ancient Egyptian was to live again in the afterlife. Tutankhamun, a young king who ruled for only a short time at a pivotal moment in Egyptian history, has become, in effect, the human face of ancient Egypt in all its glory, complexity, and richness. The gold mask that was placed over the head of his mummy has been transformed into an icon of Egyptian art and a symbol of the wealth of the pharaohs. Nevertheless, it remains a very intimate and personal item, which, to this day, allows us to look upon the face of the young king and to feel a connection to him as well as to his world.

78. (Opposite): Gold mask of Tutankhamun

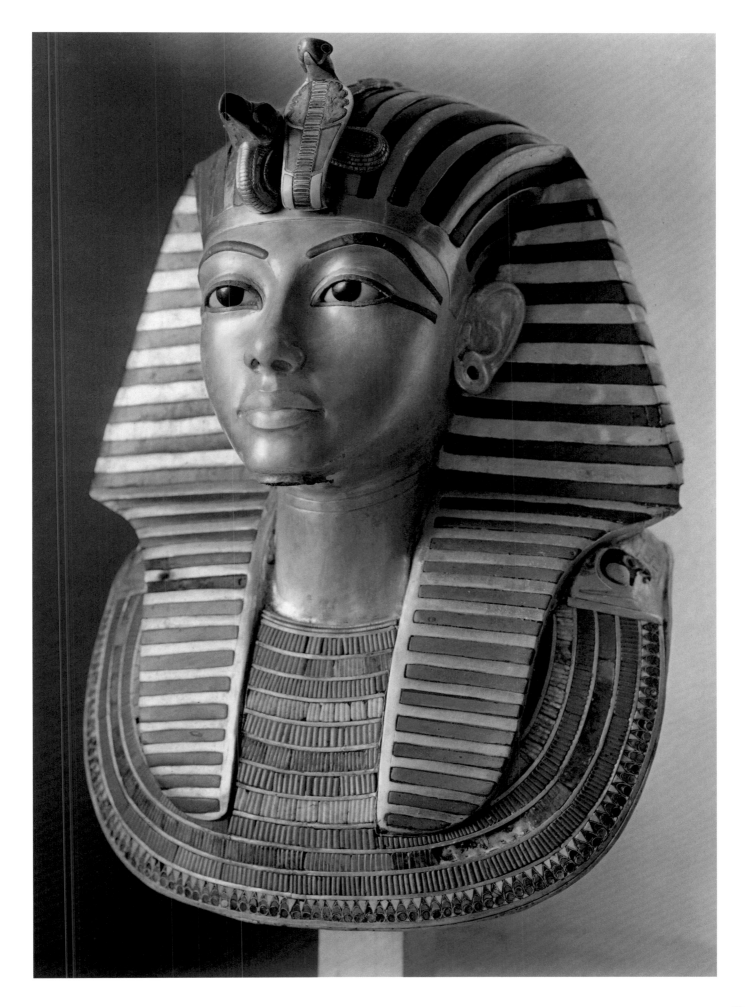

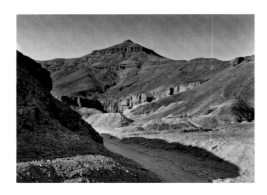

1. The entrance to the Valley of the Kings, Thebes, the burial place of the kings of ancient Egypt during the New Kingdom. The valley is dominated by a pyramid-like mountain called the Qurn. (MMA Burton photo TAA970)

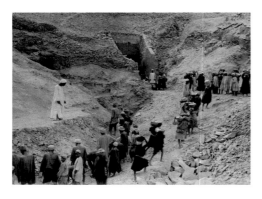

2. Carter and his Egyptian workmen spent six seasons in the Valley of the Kings, methodically clearing away limestone debris—which had accumulated from the construction of other royal tombs—until they reached bedrock. The debris was loaded into baskets and emptied into small railroad cars, like those used in mines, which transported it to a dumping ground. Finally, in the 1922 season only an area below the tomb of Ramesses VI remained to be explored. (Griffith Institute photo XXXVI)

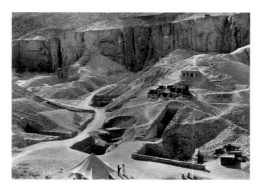

3. The site of the tomb of Tutankhamun (KV 62) after excavation. Tutankhamun's tomb, which lies below and to the right of the large entrance to the tomb of Ramesses VI (1143–1136 B.C.), had been hidden by workmen's huts and construction debris from the later tomb. Crates for the finds

from Tutankhamun's tomb can be seen at the lower right. (MMA Burton photo TAA2)

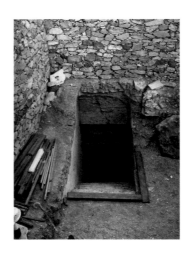

4. The mouth of the tomb after the debris was cleared away. A retaining wall was built to prevent rubble from the slope above from falling into the tomb. The white stone in the corner of this wall bears the crest of Lord Carnarvon, two interlocked Cs, and numbers that are keyed to Carter's map of the valley. (MMA Burton photo TAA3)

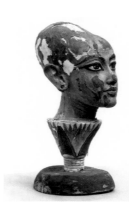

5. The painted-wood head of Tutankhamun depicts him as a young child, emerging from a lily. This head was found at the end of the entrance corridor just outside the Antechamber of the tomb. It was probably placed there deliberately and was intended to symbolize the reborn king emerging from his tomb. (MMA Burton photo TAA469)

6. The entrance passage to the tomb was originally filled with large jars that contained the remains of the funerary banquet as well as material—linen and natron—which had been used in the embalming of the body of Tutankhamun. After the tomb was robbed for the first time, these jars were removed to a nearby pit (KV 54) and the corridor filled with rubble. The discovery of the so-called embalmer's cache of Tutankhamun was one of the clues used by Carter to locate the

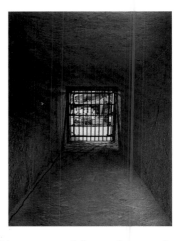

probable position of the tomb. Items from this cache came to the Metropolitan Museum in 1909 from the bequest of Theodore M. Davis, who had discovered it in 1907. (Griffith Institute Burton photo P0005)

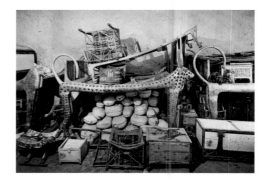

7. Three gilded and inlaid ritual couches, as well as other items of furniture and boxes, were arranged along the west wall of the Antechamber. These massive animal-headed couches were the first objects seen by Carter as he peered through the small hole that he made in the blocked doorway. Under the middle couch, which represents the cow goddess Mehetweret, were forty-eight whitewashed, wood boxes containing joints of meat. (MMA Burton photo TAA9)

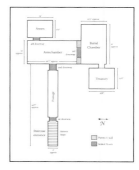

8. The plan of Tutankhamun's tomb differs from that of royal tombs of the time, both in size and in layout. It did, however, contain all the necessary ritual spaces, but only the Burial Chamber was decorated.

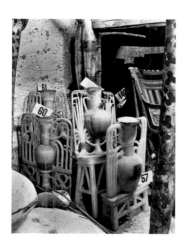

9. These four ointment jars of Egyptian alabaster (calcite), with attached stands, had been placed below one of the ritual couches along the west wall of the Antechamber. The elaborate handles of the jars are in the form of lily and papyrus plants, and represent the hieroglyph for the unification of Upper and Lower Egypt. (MMA Burton photo TAA21)

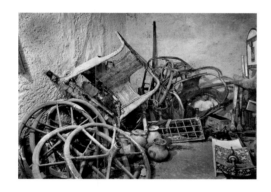

10. Four of the six dismantled chariots from the tomb, as they were found, piled up at the south end of the Antechamber. A number of alabaster ointment jars as well as two stools and the wood half-length bust of the king are also visible in the picture. (MMA Burton photo TAA11)

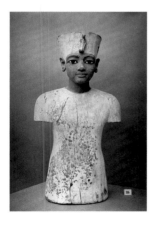

11. This wood half-length bust of the young king shows him wearing a simple tunic and the flat-topped crown with a uraeus. Carter believed

that the mannequin might have been used as a tailor's dummy for the fitting of the king's clothing and jewelry, but more likely is that the bust served some funerary purpose. (MMA Burton photo TAA499)

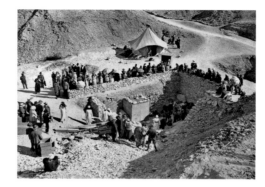

12. News of the discovery of the tomb quickly spread worldwide, and Lord Carnarvon signed an exclusive agreement with the London *Times* to control the crowds of reporters and photographers that besieged the excavation. Visitors lined up daily in the Valley, surrounding the retaining wall that had been built around the tomb entrance, and waited eagerly for Carter or for finds to emerge from the tomb. Important visitors also had to be accommodated. Here, Elisabeth, Queen of the Belgians, who was an ardent Egyptophile, visited the tomb in the company of Lord Carnarvon and his daughter Lady Evelyn Herbert. (MMA Burton photo TT1102)

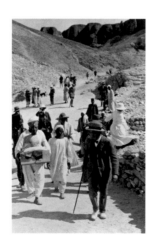

13. Once removed from the tomb, objects had to be transferred to the field laboratory in the nearby tomb of Seti II, under guard—here, followed by a procession of tourists. Between 1922 and 1926, some twelve thousand tourists thronged the Valley daily to watch as objects were brought out of the tomb. (MMA photo M57397; photographer Lindsey Hall)

14. The difficult task of removing objects from the tomb was usually performed by Carter and his assistants. Items such as this delicate chariot body

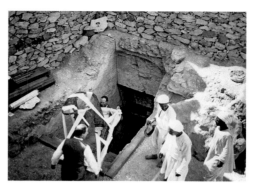

of gilded wood and leather had to be carefully padded and secured to specially built litters that were maneuvered through the low, narrow entrance passageway and up to the surface. (MMA photo M57388; photographer Lindsey Hall)

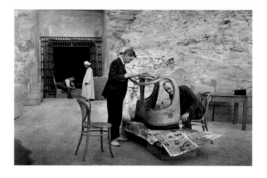

15. Arthur Mace (standing, at the left) and Alfred Lucas (seated, at the right) cleaning and securing the surface of one of the chariots. The nearby tomb of Seti II was converted into a laboratory for the repair and conservation of the objects from the tomb before they were packed for shipment to the Egyptian Museum in Cairo. Mace, an archaeologist with considerable experience in the treatment and reconstruction of fragile objects, had worked for the Metropolitan Museum since 1907. Lucas was a research chemist, who wrote the first book on ancient Egyptian materials. (MMA Burton photo TAA315)

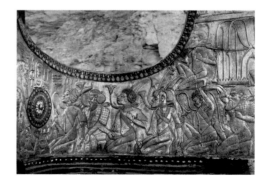

16. This section of a chariot body shows a group of bound prisoners facing a large inlaid rosette and the king in the form of a sphinx at the far left. The prisoners are tied together by the papyrus-and-lotus-plant tendrils that issue from the

unification sign at the upper right. The highly detailed costume and hairstyle of each of the prisoners, who represent the traditional African, Near Eastern, and Libyan enemies of Egypt, are carefully depicted. (MMA Burton photo TAA322)

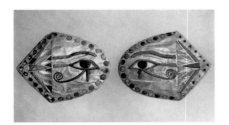

17. This pair of wood horse blinders, overlaid with sheet gold and inlaid with colored glass, depicts the protective *udjat*, or eyes of Horus, and lotus blossoms. They were found among the dismantled chariots in the Antechamber and formed part of the harnesses and other equipment. (MMA Burton photo TAA334)

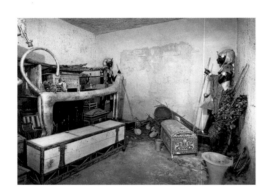

18. The north wall of the Antechamber, showing the still-sealed entrance to the Burial Chamber. On either side of the doorway are two guardian statues of the king in wood, painted black and gilded. The famous Painted Box, decorated with scenes of the young king hunting and in battle, is seen in front of the door. (MMA Burton photo TAA4)

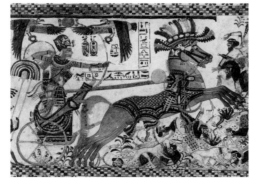

19. On this side panel of the Painted Box, Tutankhamun is depicted in battle with the Syrians. He is shown in a decorated chariot similar to those found in the tomb. The Syrians,

pierced by the king's arrows, tumble beneath the hooves of his horses and are attacked by his dogs. The landscape of Syria is indicated by the plants beneath the chariot wheels. (MMA Burton photo TAA961)

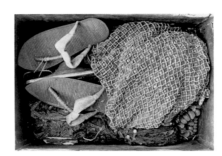

20. More than fifty items of the king's personal clothing and regalia were found inside the Painted Box. Uppermost was a simple pair of papyrus-and-rush sandals. Much of the fabric in the tomb was in poor condition; the elaborate beaded robe seen here soon disintegrated. (MMA Burton photo TAA193)

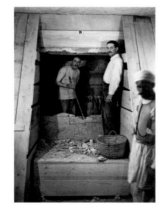

21. Howard Carter is visible behind the partly demolished blocking of the entrance to the Burial Chamber. Archaeologist Arthur Mace stands outside, in the Antechamber, in front of the wood put in place to protect the guardian statues of the king, which flank the doorway. (Griffith Institute Burton photo P0290)

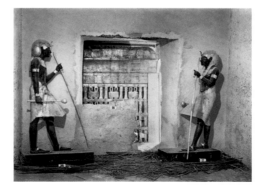

22. A view into the Burial Chamber, with the doorway still partially blocked. The outermost

gilded wood shrine erected over the sarcophagus is visible. The bands of *djed* pillars and the *tyet* signs that decorate the exterior of the shrine are symbols of longevity and protection. (MMA Burton photo TAA616)

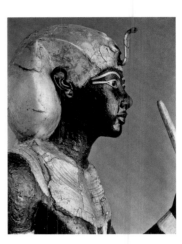

23. One of the two life-size wood statues of the deceased king that flanked the sealed entrance to the Burial Chamber. He is depicted standing, holding a staff, and wears a bag wig decorated with a uraeus. His eyes and eyebrows are inlaid with limestone and obsidian and ringed with gilded bronze; his wig, broad collar, kilt, armlets, and sandals are all covered in gesso and gilded. The black skin of the pharaoh is painted resin, applied directly over the wood, and identifies him with Osiris, god of the netherworld. (MMA Burton photo TAA720)

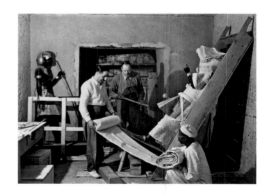

24. Howard Carter, together with Arthur Callender, a retired engineer and architect and his longtime friend, wraps one of the two guardian statues for transport. It is estimated that a mile of cotton wadding and thirty-two bales of cloth were used to pack the objects from the Antechamber alone. (MMA Burton photo TAA715)

25. Arthur Mace (standing) had participated in The Metropolitan Museum of Art Egyptian Expedition excavations since their inception in 1907. Alfred Lucas (seated) was a pioneer in the field of archaeological chemistry in Egypt. Here, the two men clean and treat one of the guardian

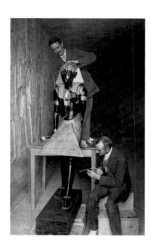

statues of the king in the field laboratory set up in the nearby tomb of Seti II. (Griffith Institute Burton photo P493)

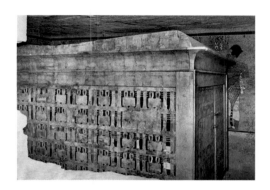

26. The outermost shrine in the Burial Chamber is seen through the still partly blocked doorway. The shrine is made of hardwood overlaid with gesso and thin sheet gold and inlaid with blue faience. Almost nine feet tall, it was composed of twenty separate pieces. A wall painting depicting the funeral rites of Tutankhamun is partially visible in the background. (MMA Burton photo TAA674)

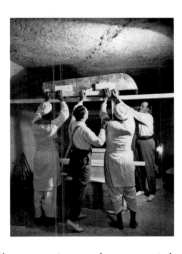

27. The excavation work was carried out in the hot, dusty, and ill-ventilated tomb, where barely three feet separated the outermost shrine from the walls of the Burial Chamber. Arthur Callender's engineering skills proved especially

useful in lifting and removing often massive—but delicate—objects in confined spaces. (Griffith Institute Burton photo P0605)

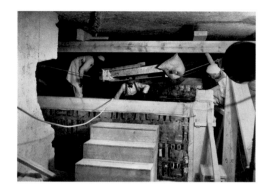

28. Scaffolds and pulleys had to be rigged to lift and maneuver parts of the shrines. (Griffith Institute Burton photo P0634)

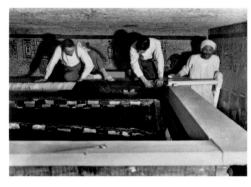

29. Once the roof of the outermost shrine was removed, a delicate linen pall, sewn with heavy gilt-bronze rosettes, was found resting on a framework over the second shrine. Extremely fragile, it could not be lifted intact. Here, Carter and Mace carefully roll the linen around a padded pole. (Griffith Institute Burton photo P0619)

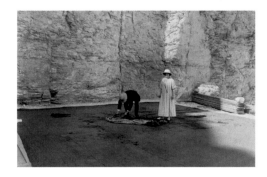

30. Like most of the textiles in the tomb, the linen pall was in very poor condition. Egyptologist Percy Newberry and his wife attempt to spread it out on a large area that has been covered with fabric. (Griffith Institute Burton photo P0622)

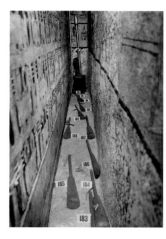

31. Placed against the north wall of the Burial Chamber, between the wall and the outermost shrine, were an Anubis fetish (pl. 33), a double wood shrine containing blue faience cups, and eleven magical oars. The oars were coated with black resin and the blades were decorated with yellow *udjat* eyes. These oars are similar to the large steering oars often seen in tomb paintings and on models of boats. (MMA Burton photo TAA40)

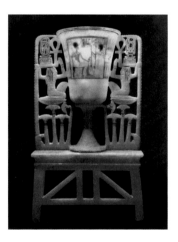

32. This elaborate Egyptian alabaster lamp is in the form of a tall chalice on a stand. It is flanked by two panels of openwork papyrus plants that support the god Heh, on top of which are the king's cartouche and an ankh sign. The chalice itself is composed of two cups, one fitted inside the other, and is decorated with a scene of the queen presenting an offering to the seated king. The translucent character of the stone allowed the scene to be visible when the lamp was lit, as it is in this photograph. Traces of oil were found in the bowl of the lamp. (MMA Burton photo TAA487)

33. These two gilded wood Anubis fetishes had been placed in the northwest and southwest corners of the Burial Chamber. They represent the skin of an animal attached to a pole terminating in a lily bud and are set in an Egyptian alabaster vessel inscribed with the names and titles of the

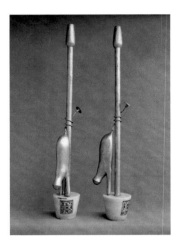

king and the epithet, "Beloved of Anubis who presides over the embalming booth." Anubis was the jackal-headed god of embalming. (MMA Burton photo TAA91)

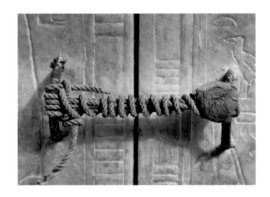

34. The doors of the second shrine were secured by an unbroken closure made by passing a cord around two copper rings and then knotting it. Over the cord a clay sealing—with the official seal of the necropolis, a jackal over the Nine Bows—was applied. The jackal represents Anubis, protector of the cemetery, and the kneeling, bound captives symbolize the traditional enemies of Egypt. (MMA Burton photo TAA622)

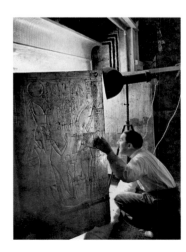

35. Howard Carter looks through the doors of the second shrine. The gold foil covering the leaf of the door is incised in low relief with a

beautifully executed scene of the pharaoh before the god Osiris. All of the shrines were inscribed inside and out with spells from the Book of the Dead and other religious texts. The doors of the shrines open to the east, toward the rising sun. (MMA Burton photo TAA678)

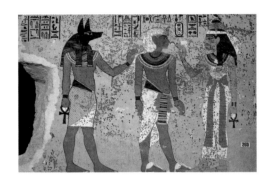

36. The south wall of the Burial Chamber was decorated very simply with figures of the king and various gods. Here, the goddess Hathor, Mistress of the West, offers the ankh, the symbol of life, to the king, who is accompanied by Anubis, god of the necropolis. The wall of the Burial Chamber, seen at the left in the photograph, had to be broken away in order to remove the large gilded shrines. The small number at the right indicates the location of one of the plastered niches in which the magic bricks and figures were found. (MMA Burton photo TAA50)

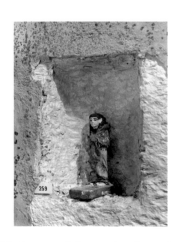

37. This is one of four painted-wood figures that were placed in specially prepared niches in the walls of the Burial Chamber. Each figure stands on an inscribed magic brick, and is swathed in linen. The niches were closed with large flakes of limestone, plastered over, and their surfaces painted to match the rest of the wall decoration. (MMA Burton photo TAA495)

38 and 39. During the period when the tomb was being cleared, which lasted from 1922 to 1933, it had to be sealed and the staircase refilled at the end of each working season to secure it against modern grave robbers. (London *Times*)

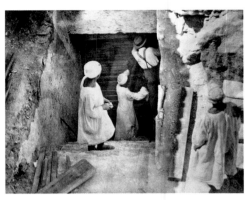

38

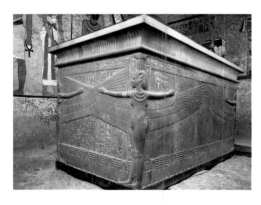

39

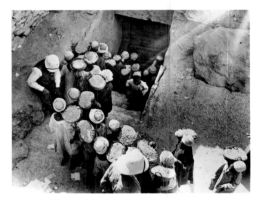

40. The red quartzite sarcophagus of the king, nine feet long and almost five feet high, was carved from a single block of stone. At each corner a goddess—here, Nephthys—with outstretched wings guards the mummy. Around the base is a frieze of ankhs and of *djed* pillars, and a cavetto cornice supports the lid. The inscriptions are invocations by the gods of ancient Egypt for the protection and well-being of the pharaoh in the afterlife. (MMA Burton photo TAA864)

41. The face of the outer coffin of Tutankhamun is made of cypress, overlaid with gesso and gold foil, and is covered with feathered decoration in low relief. A small wreath of olive leaves and

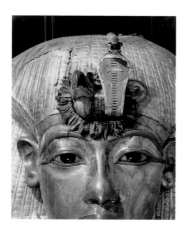

flowers is still in place over the vulture, the symbol of Upper Egypt, and the uraeus, the symbol of Lower Egypt, on the forehead of the king. (MMA Burton photo TAA364)

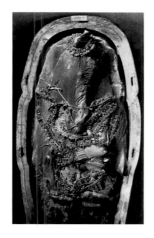

42. The second coffin of the king is seen covered with a linen shroud. Floral garlands were draped over the body and a small wreath was placed on the forehead. The composition of the garlands—willow and olive leaves, wild celery, lilies, and cornflowers—seems to indicate that Tutankhamun was buried in spring. (MMA Burton photo TAA368)

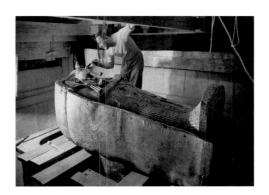

43. Carter, brush in hand, detaches fragments of the decayed linen shroud (see pl. 42), which covered the second coffin. The nested coffins

were lifted from the sarcophagus in one piece and rest on thick planks placed on top of its rim. In order to remove the stone lid of the sarcophagus and the extremely heavy coffins, the shrines had to be dismantled and strong beams and pulleys positioned over the sarcophagus. (MMA Burton photo TAA371)

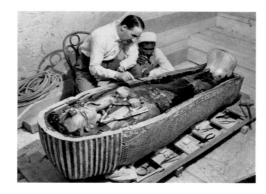

44. Carter and one of his workmen examine the third innermost coffin of the king, which is made of solid gold and still rests inside the second coffin. The black substance on its surface is aromatic resin that had been poured over the inner coffin during the funeral ceremonies, and had hardened, making it very difficult to separate the gold coffin from the second one. (MMA Burton photo TAA1354)

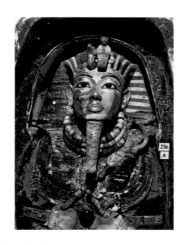

45. The gold mask of Tutankhamun is shown as it was found on his mummy, still covered with the resins and ointments that were poured over it; these had hardened and darkened. Several pieces of jewelry, including a black resin scarab, and hands of sheet gold, which adorned the mummy, are also visible. (MMA Burton photo TAA512)

46. Howard Carter and Douglas Derry, a British anatomist, in the tomb of Seti II (KV15), examine the mummy of Tutankhamun in the presence of Pierre Lacau, director of the Egyptian

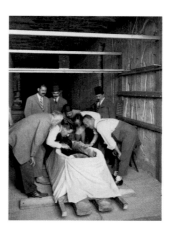

Antiquities Service, and a group of Egyptian doctors and officials. (MMA Burton photo TAA1103)

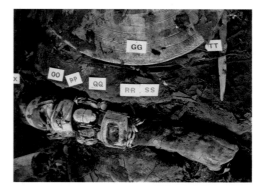

47. Visible here are the chest and arms of the mummy, with the gold, broad collar and the bracelets still in place. The heavily decayed and blackened condition of the linen wrappings is apparent as well. Whether this decay was due to the copious amounts of resins and ointments applied to the mummy or to the conditions in the tomb after burial is not clear. (MMA Burton photo TAA522)

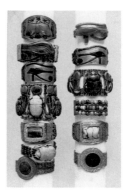

48. Thirteen bracelets were found on the forearms of the mummy, seven on the right arm (seen in pl. 47 in situ) and six on the left. Several of the bracelets include scarabs separated by motifs such as uraei and ankhs; some have a large amuletic *udjat* eye or another central element. The bracelets were made of gold, multicolored glass, faience, and semiprecious stones. (MMA Burton photo TAA1382)

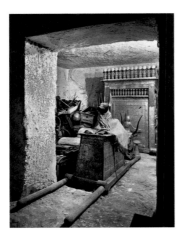

49. The statue of Anubis, god of the dead, rests atop a portable shrine at the entrance to the Treasury. Behind it stands the canopic shrine of Tutankhamun (pl. 57) and the head and horns of the goddess Hathor, as a cow (pl. 51). The doorway between the Burial Chamber and the Treasury was not sealed in antiquity. (MMA Burton photo TAA55)

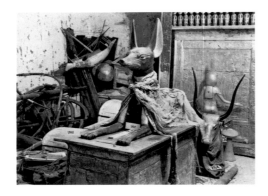

50. A close-up view of the figure of Anubis shows him still robed in a fringed linen tunic, or shirt, with streamers. Behind him are boxes, chariots, a model boat, a head of Hathor as a cow, and, at the back, the massive gilded canopic shrine. (MMA Burton photo TAA1004)

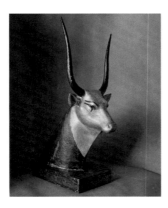

51. This head of a cow—made of wood, over-laid with gesso, gilded, and varnished with resin—was found in the Treasury directly behind the portable shrine of Anubis and in front of the gilded canopic shrine. It represents the goddess Hathor, Mistress of the West. (MMA Burton photo TAA410)

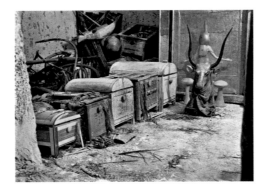

52. This view of the Treasury with the shrine of Anubis removed shows a row of five elaborately decorated chests that contained more of the personal possessions of the king. The lids, which are askew, and the scraps of linen are indications that the chests had been rifled by tomb robbers. The boxes were originally secured by winding a cord around the knobs on the ends and on the lids and applying a stamped clay sealing. Fragments of these sealings were found on the floor beneath the boxes. Behind the gilded head of Hathor are two Egyptian alabaster offering stands with matching lids. (Griffith Institute Burton photo P1175)

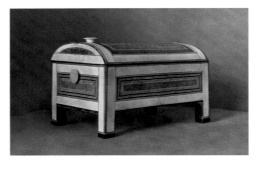

53. This round-topped wood chest is veneered with strips of ivory and decorated with marquetry panels of ivory and ebony. The minute inlays—Carter estimated that there were some forty-seven thousand pieces—are set in herringbone, crisscross, and diamond patterns. (MMA Burton photo TAA224)

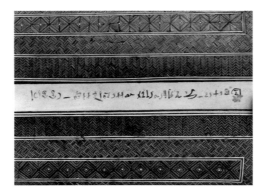

54. A detail of the lid of the chest in plate 53 shows the intricacy of the inlaid ivory-and-ebony marquetry patterns. An inscription in hieratic (the cursive form of hieroglyphs) across

the top of the lid can be read as "Jewels of gold of the procession made in the bed-chamber of Nebkheperure" (the prenomen of Tutankhamun). The box did, indeed, contain some of the king's jewelry. (MMA Burton photo TAA1037)

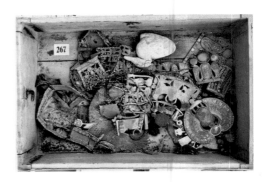

55. The contents of the ivory-and-ebony chest appear here as found. Most of the jewelry was probably originally tied up in linen bundles, which were then sealed. There were some sixteen separate necklaces and jewelry elements in this box. (MMA Burton photo TAA224a)

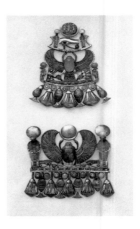

56. These two pectorals were found in the ivory-and-ebony veneered chest. Their elaborate designs, composed of many elements—winged scarabs, uraei with sun disks on their heads, *udjat* eyes, the sacred bark, lunar disks and crescents, lily and poppy flowers, and papyrus heads—were intended to convey a very complex religious symbolism. The pectorals are made of gold, silver, and electrum, and are inlaid with semiprecious stones, including carnelian, lapis lazuli, turquoise, chalcedony, feldspar, calcite, obsidian, as well as colored glass. (MMA Burton photo TAA578)

57. The canopic shrine of Tutankhamun is in the form of a gilded wood box mounted on a sledge and placed within a canopy crowned with an elaborate frieze of uraei, inlaid with glass and faience, bearing sun disks on their heads. The shrine stands more than six feet tall. Each

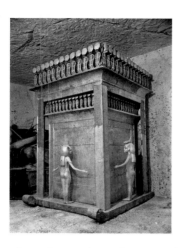

side is four feet wide and is guarded by the figure of a goddess with her arms outstretched in protection. The goddess Selket, with a scorpion on her head, is at the right, and the goddess Isis is at the left. (MMA Burton photo TAA269)

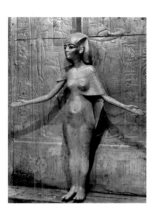

58. This statuette of the goddess Isis depicts her wearing a delicately pleated, closely fitting dress, and a shawl draped over her shoulders. Her symbol, the throne, sits atop her head. Like the winged goddesses at the corners of the pharaoh's sarcophagus (pl. 40), her arms are outstretched. Her head is turned slightly to one side, breaking a basic rule of ancient Egyptian art that statues in the round always must always face front. (MMA Burton photo TAA968)

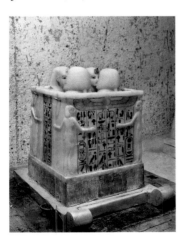

59. The canopic chest of Tutankhamun was carved from a single block of Egyptian alabaster (calcite). A goddess stands at each corner, and

her words of protection are inscribed on the four sides of the box. The chest is shown here with its lid removed, revealing the four heads of the king that covered the four compartments containing his internal organs. Each head wears the striped headcloth, or *nemes* headdress, adorned with the vulture and uraeus ornaments on the brow. Details are picked out in red and black. It is probable that this chest was made for one of Tutankhamun's predecessors, the female pharaoh Neferneferuaten, as were a number of other objects in the tomb (see plates 40, 60). (MMA Burton photo TAA281)

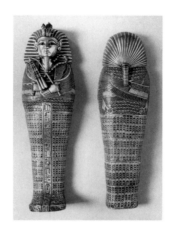

60. These elaborately detailed, miniature gold canopic coffins, inlaid with glass and semiprecious stones, are masterpieces of the goldsmith's art. The coffins are covered with a feather pattern and the interiors are inscribed with spells. They were placed inside the compartments of the alabaster canopic chest, to contain the mummified viscera of the king. The erasure of the name of Neferneferuaten and its replacement with that of Tutankhamun on these coffins indicates that, like the Egyptian alabaster heads of the canopic box, this canopic equipment was originally intended for another royal burial. (MMA Burton photo TAA1340)

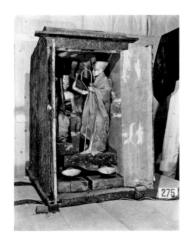

61. One of the small wood shrines found in the Treasury is shown here with the doors open, revealing five gilded wood statuettes of

Tutankhamun wrapped in linen. The statue visible in front depicts the king holding a crook and wearing the Red Crown of Lower Egypt; two other statuettes behind that of the king stand on small papyrus boats and raise harpoons to spear a hippopotamus, a symbol of chaos in ancient Egyptian society. (MMA Burton photo TAA685)

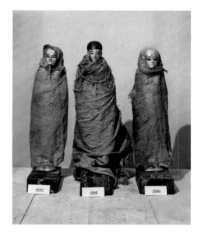

62. Each of these three wood statuettes of gods was found in a wood shrine box in the Treasury. All are still swathed in linen. On the left is Tatenen, an earth god and protector of the deceased king in the netherworld; in the center is Ptah, the creator; and on the right is Atum, the god from whom all other gods were created. (MMA Burton photo TAA702)

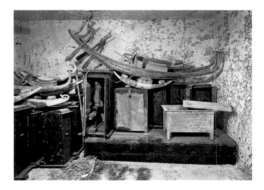

63. A view of the Treasury showing some of the eighteen large model boats and twenty-four wood shrines filled with statuettes. The doors of one shrine are open, revealing two statuettes still wrapped in linen, each depicting the king standing on the back of a black leopard. The large, flat wood box under the shrines and boats contains the so-called Osiris bed: a wood frame more than six feet long; it was filled with earth and sown with grain intended to germinate in the dark tomb to symbolize the resurrection both of Osiris and of the dead king. The prows of the boats all face west—the direction of the journey into the netherworld. (MMA Burton photo TAA1009)

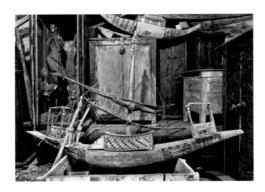

64. This fully rigged model of a sailing boat is made of painted wood and has linen sails. The boat itself is in the form of a papyrus skiff: in the center is a cabin with steps leading to the roof, and the checkered sides imitate painted leather. At each end of the boat are pavilions where the king could sit to enjoy the breezes. As this is an upstream boat, the two steering oars are meant to act as rudders. The boat rests on top of a wood model of a granary; behind it are numerous boxes containing ritual figures of the king and of various gods. (MMA Burton photo TAA65)

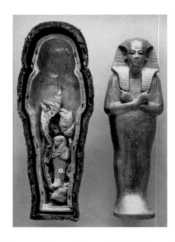

65. This set of nested model coffins, of gilded wood, was found in the Treasury. Inside was a miniature wood coffin that, in turn, held an even smaller coffin-shaped box inscribed with the name of Queen Tiye, who was the wife of Amenhotep III, and probably the grandmother of Tutankhamun. Within this box was a lock of her hair. A linen bundle also placed in the model coffins contained a gold necklace and a pendant depicting the king as a squatting child. (MMA Burton photo TAA387)

66. This small gold pendant in the form of a squatting child king, found wrapped in linen inside the nested miniature coffins, was strung on a heavy woven gold chain. The figure wears the Blue Crown and holds a scepter and flail, the insignia of an Egyptian pharaoh (see pl. 70), casually against his shoulder. His feet are bare and around his neck is a string of tiny colored beads. This exquisitely detailed statuette is only two inches high and has no parallel. Carter believed that the child represented

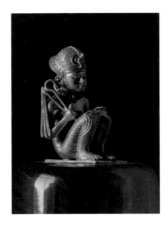

Amenhotep III, who was probably Tutankhamun's grandfather, but the inscriptions on the nested coffins mention only Tutankhamun. Moreover, the figure's earlobes are pierced for large earrings—a feature not seen on representations of the king before the time of Akhenaten. (MMA Burton photo TAA1214)

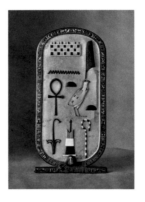

67. This elaborately decorated and inscribed wood box is in the shape of the cartouche of Tutankhamun. The borders of the cartouche, the knob, and some of the hieroglyphs are made of ebony; the remaining hieroglyphs are of ivory. All of these elements are applied to a gilded background. The band around the rim is inscribed with the names and epithets of the king, while the large hieroglyphs may be read as "Tutankhamun, the Ruler of Southern Heliopolis" [Thebes, or modern-day Luxor]. (MMA Burton photo TAA231)

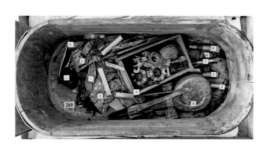

68. The cartouche-shaped box is shown as it appeared when found, with a small box of jewelry, a gilded mirror case in the shape of an ankh, and two pairs of scepters and flails inside

(pl. 70). Since the cartouche-shaped box was discovered in the Treasury and was partially plundered by tomb robbers, it is uncertain if all the items it contained represented its original contents or were placed there by the priests who tried to restore order in the tomb after the robbery. (MMA Burton photo TAA232)

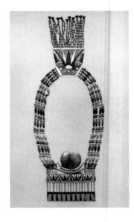

69. This magnificent necklace, part of the personal jewelry of the king, was found in the cartouche-shaped box (pl. 67). Made of gold, electrum, lapis lazuli, carnelian, and feldspar, it employs complex hieroglyphic imagery. On the pectoral, the lunar disk is borne by the sacred bark across the night sky. A cloisonné counterweight with lilies and beaded tassels balances the heavy pectoral. (MMA Burton photo TAA1387)

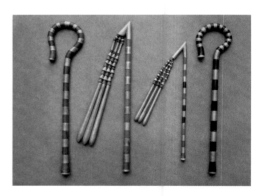

70. The *heqa* scepter, in the shape of a crook, and the flail, or fly whisk, are the traditional royal insignia of the pharaoh. These two pairs of scepters and flails, discovered in the king's cartouche-shaped box (pl. 67), are constructed of alternating cylindrical segments of blue glass, obsidian, and gold, over a copper or wood core. The beads of the flail are made of gilded wood. On statues and representations of the pharaoh, he holds the scepter and flail crossed over his chest. Similar pairs of scepters and flails are shown on all three coffins and on the four canopic coffins of Tutankhamun, and another pair was found on his mummy. (MMA Burton photo TAA609)

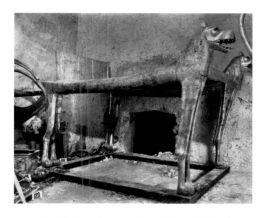

71. After all the objects placed beneath the large ritual couch had been removed, the opening in the west wall of the Antechamber leading into the Annex was revealed. Despite having been sealed and blocked by tomb equipment, the entrance to this storeroom was located and broken into by tomb robbers. (MMA Burton photo TAA408)

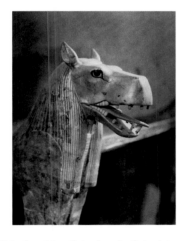

72. This detail is of the head of the hippopotamus goddess from one of the gilded ritual couches in the Antechamber (pl. 71). The composite creature has the body of a lion and the tail of a crocodile. Her fierce aspect is emphasized by her open mouth with its ivory teeth and tongue, the latter stained red. (MMA Burton photo TAA409)

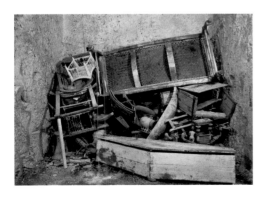

73. Furniture—a bed and chairs—as well as boxes, baskets, alabaster and pottery vessels, and model boats were piled up at the north end of

the Annex. The oddly shaped white box held the pharaoh's bows. The Annex, the last room to be cleared by Howard Carter in 1927, contained more than 283 groups of objects. It was originally intended for the storage of foodstuffs in baskets, oils and ointments, pottery jars, and stone vessels. (MMA Burton photo TAA83)

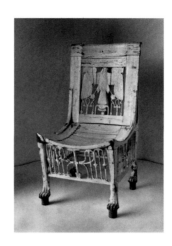

74. Tossed unceremoniously on top of the pile of furniture in the Annex, this white painted-wood chair was well preserved. The legs of the chair are feline in form and the stretchers display the *sema-tawy* sign, emblematic of the unification of Upper and Lower Egypt. The openwork carving on the back of the chair represents a falcon with outstretched wings resting on hieroglyphic signs. The falcon is the symbol of the god Horus, and the living king was the embodiment of this god. Two cartouches of the king are placed above the falcon's wings, and in his claws he holds the signs for eternity. (MMA Burton photo TAA1268)

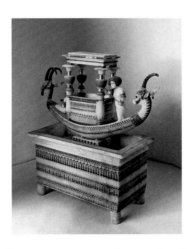

75. The many extravagantly carved and decorated stone and alabaster vessels found in the tomb usually were lamps or containers for ointments. This object seems to have served no function other than a decorative or symbolic one. A boat in the form of a papyrus skiff, with ibex-headed terminals, carved of Egyptian

alabaster and inlaid with colored pigments and gold, rests on a pylon-like base with a cavetto cornice. The base is recessed to indicate a pool. On the boat, a nude young woman holding a lotus sits before an elaborate floral pavilion. At the back of the boat, a nude female dwarf grasps a steering or punting pole. (MMA Burton photo TAA1064)

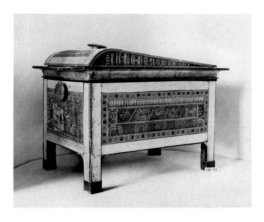

76. This wood-and-ivory veneered box is in the form of a shrine, with a cavetto cornice and a sloping lid. The box is elaborately decorated with ivory, ebony, faience, glass, and alabaster inlays, in panels whose highly stylized and densely patterned scenes show the king hunting animals in a landscape. On the top of the box is a panel depicting the young king and queen (pl. 77). (MMA Burton photo TAA947)

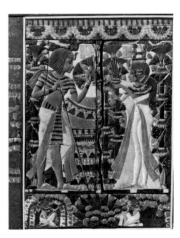

77. This carved-and-painted ivory panel is from the lid of a box found in the Annex. It shows the young queen, Ankhesenamun, offering a bouquet to her husband, Tutankhamun, who leans on his staff. They stand in a vine-draped pavilion; the background, border, and panel below are all filled with dense floral and fruit motifs. The relaxed pose of the king and couple's slightly smiling faces lend the scene a special intimacy. (MMA Burton photo TAA249)

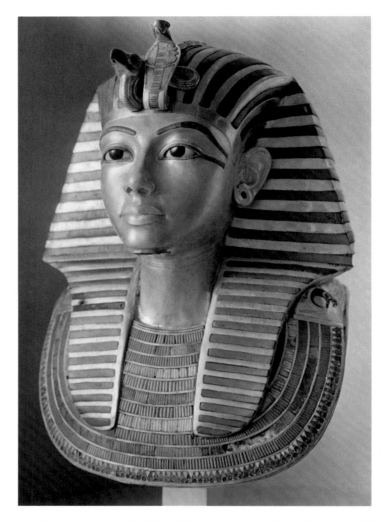

78. The mummy mask of Tutankhamun is made of two sheets of solid gold inlaid with glass, faience, and semiprecious stones, and weighs twenty-two-and-a-half pounds. The pharaoh wears the striped head-cloth, or *nemes* headdress, adorned with the vulture and uraeus, and a broad collar with falcon-headed terminals. A false beard, emblematic of his divinity (visible in pl. 45), is not included here. (MMA Burton photo TAA505)

Suggested Reading

All of the photographs taken by Harry Burton in the tomb of Tutankhamun, as well as Howard Carter's notes and excavation records, can be found on the Griffith Institute website, Tutankhamun: Anatomy of an Excavation http://www.ashmolean.museum/gri/4tut.html

Arnold, D. *The Royal Women of Amarna: Images of Beauty from Ancient Egypt.* New York, 1996.

Carter, H. E., and A. C. Mace. *The Tomb of Tut·ankh·amen, Discovered by the Late Earl of Carnarvon and Howard Carter.* 3 vols. New York, 1923–33.

Eaton-Krauss, M. *The Sarcophagus from the Tomb of Tutankhamun.* Oxford, 1985.

Eaton-Krauss, M., and E. Graefe. *The Small Golden Shrine from the Tomb of Tutankhamun.* Oxford, 1985.

Edwards, I. E. S. *Tutankhamun: His Tomb and Its Treasures.* New York, 1976.

Hawass, Z. *Tutankhamun and the Golden Age of the Pharaohs.* Washington, D.C., 2005.

Johnson, G. B. "Painting with Light: The Work of Harry Burton, Archaeological Photographer," with a biographical essay by Marsha Hill. *KMT* 8:2 (Spring 1997), pp. 58–77.

el-Khouli, A., R. Holthoer, C. A. Hope, and O. E. Kaper. *Stone Vessels, Pottery and Sealings from the Tomb of Tutankhamun.* Oxford, 1994.

The Metropolitan Museum of Art. *Wonderful Things: The Discovery of Tutankhamun's Tomb.* New York, 1976.

Reeves, C. N. *The Complete Tutankhamun: The King, the Tomb, the Royal Treasure.* London, 1995.

Tutankhamun's Tomb Series. Griffith Institute, Oxford, 1963–

No. 1. H. Murray and M. Nuttall. *A Handlist of Howard Carter's Catalogue of Objects in Tutankhamun's Tomb.* 1963.

No. 2. J. Černý. *Hieratic Inscriptions from the Tomb of Tutankhamun.* 1965.

No. 3. W. McLeod. *Composite Bows from the Tomb of Tutankhamun.* 1970.

No. 4. W. McLeod. *Self Bows and Other Archery Tackle from the Tomb of Tutankhamun.* 1982.

No. 5. F. Filce Leek. *The Human Remains from the Tomb of Tutankhamun.* 1972.

No. 6. L. Manniche. *Musical Instruments from the Tomb of Tutankhamun.* 1976.

No. 7. W. J. Tait. *Game Boxes and Accessories from the Tomb of Tutankhamun.* 1982.

No. 8. M. A. Littauer and J. H. Crouwel. *Chariots and Related Equipment from the Tomb of Tutankhamun.* 1985.

No. 9. D. Jones. *Model Boats from the Tomb of Tutankhamun.* 1990.